Bloom
WHERE YOU'RE PLANTED

Mary Rodman

WESTBOW
P R E S S®
A DIVISION OF THOMAS NELSON
& ZONDERVAN

Unless otherwise indicated, all Scripture quotations are taken from the Holy Bible, New Living Translation, copyright © 1996, 2004, 2007 by Tyndale House Foundation. Used by permission of Tyndale House Publishers, Inc., Carol Stream, Illinois 60188. All rights reserved.

Scripture quotations marked (NIV) are taken from the Holy Bible, New International Version®, NIV®. Copyright © 1973, 1978, 1984, 2011 by Biblica, Inc.™ Used by permission of Zondervan. All rights reserved worldwide. www.zondervan.com The "NIV" and "New International Version" are trademarks registered in the United States Patent and Trademark Office by Biblica, Inc.™

Scripture taken from the NEW AMERICAN STANDARD BIBLE®, Copyright © 1960,1962,1963,1968,1971,1972,1973,1975,1977,1 995 by The Lockman Foundation. Used by permission.

Scripture taken from The Message. Copyright © 1993, 1994, 1995, 1996, 2000, 2001, 2002. Used by permission of NavPress Publishing Group.

WestBow Press books may be ordered through booksellers or by contacting:

WestBow Press
A Division of Thomas Nelson & Zondervan
1663 Liberty Drive
Bloomington, IN 47403
www.westbowpress.com
1 (866) 928-1240

Because of the dynamic nature of the Internet, any web addresses or links contained in this book may have changed since publication and may no longer be valid. The views expressed in this work are solely those of the author and do not necessarily reflect the views of the publisher, and the publisher hereby disclaims any responsibility for them.

Any people depicted in stock imagery provided by Thinkstock are models, and such images are being used for illustrative purposes only. Certain stock imagery © Thinkstock.

ISBN: 978-1-5127-5904-4 (sc)
ISBN: 978-1-5127-5905-1 (hc)
ISBN: 978-1-5127-5903-7 (e)

Library of Congress Control Number: 2016916451

Print information available on the last page.

WestBow Press rev. date: 10/26/2016

CKNOWLEDGEMENTS

A special thank you:

To my Mom, Mildred Conklin, who taught me to make the best of every situation in life. "Bloom Where You're Planted" was the model for her life, even in her final struggles before she went home to be with Jesus.

To my Dad, Joe Conklin, who gave me every opportunity in life and taught me to never give up hope in the face of adversity.

To my wonderful husband, Jim Rodman, who has supported me throughout this project. Our life together has made this book possible, as we faced struggles and joys together for over twenty-five years.

To my son Ryan King for permission to use his devotion as part of the conclusion.

To my son Matthew King for assisting me with photo selections.

My children and grandchildren, Matt, Gina, Mya, Reagan, Ryan, Kim and Jackson who have provided me with wonderful stories. Without the family memories, many of these devotions would not have been possible.

To my Golden Girls Share Group, Rachel, Angie and Kelli for your prayers and encouragement while writing devotions. You have been a great blessing to me.

To my friend Rachel Sirca for the countless hours of proofreading and offering wonderful grammatical advice. Also thank you for taking my photo for the book.

To my friend Angie Howard for continually encouraging me to step out in faith and reminding me to never give up hope.

To Pastor Kathy Reiff for investing in me as a leader, for her spiritual guidance, and the encouragement to publish my devotions.

$\mathcal{F}$OREWORD

I like to call them God-incidents. You know, those moments where you feel the presence of God in a powerful way during your every day activity, or perhaps it's when you're having a difficult time in your life and someone unexpectedly contacts you to see how you are. Mary has a gift for looking at these God-incidents in her life, interlacing them with scripture, and putting them down on paper.

Mary and I met several years ago at a spiritual renewal weekend called, "The Walk to Emmaus," and have served together on several more of these weekends. It was during one of these "Walks" that Mary shared one of her writings with me; one of her God-incidents. Mary shared with me she had several more if I would like to read them. I was deeply touched by what she had written and how she related scripture to the events. I and several others encouraged her to continue writing and put the writings together in a book. I'm glad she listened and followed through.

One of my favorites happens to be "Bird Poop." Yes, you read right. Mary's husband, Jim, challenged her to write a devotion about bird poop and she did just that. She related how we step into those unexpected problems in our lives and we feel like we are in the midst of bird poop. I'll let you read the devotion for yourself to see how Mary has taken those God-incidents in her life, related Biblical stories and scripture to them, and woven them into the wonderful book you now hold in your hands.

When you finish reading I hope you will embrace Mary as a friend and come to see similar God-incidents in your life as well. I am proud to call Mary my friend and look forward to sharing more with her in the future.

Pastor Kathy Reiff

$\mathcal{I}$NTRODUCTION

"Bloom Where You're Planted" is a group of stories about my life and some of the lessons God taught me along the way. Life has so much to offer. Many of us wish there were only good times, but if there weren't trials in life, when would we grow? My prayer is that you will see Christ woven throughout the stories and my life. You will find an assortment which includes: Childhood memories, parenting, travels, country living, farm life, and the joys of grand-parenting. Our journey on earth offers so many twists and turns, and I always try to see God's lessons in the little things.

I find joy when a harvest is plentiful or a vacation view is breathtaking. Times like these bring me peace and great reflection upon the graciousness of Christ. At the end of the day I can rest in God's arms meditating on verses such as *Psalm 4:7–8 "You have given me greater joy than those who have abundant harvests of grain and new wine. In peace I will lie down and sleep, for you alone, O Lord, will keep me safe."*

Sometimes life offers us sorrow and pain. Though walking through the difficulties of life can be trying, it is during these times that we grow the most. God didn't promise that all our days would be filled with joy, but He did promise to always be with us. *"So be truly glad. There is wonderful joy ahead, even though you have to endure many trials for a little while. These trials will show that your faith is genuine. It is being tested as fire tests and purifies gold—though your faith is far more precious than mere gold. So when your faith remains strong through many trials, it will bring you much praise and glory and honor on the day when Jesus Christ is revealed to the whole world" (1 Peter 1:6–7).*

Solomon, in his wisdom wrote *Ecclesiastes 3:1,"For everything there is a season, a time for every activity under heaven."* This verse is true for each and every one of us. Life is filled with everything from unspeakable joy to great sorrow. The devotions which follow will show a glimpse of my life and the wonderful Hand of God as He has helped me set deep roots of faith, even in the rocky soil of life. I thank God for both the blessings and the trials in my life, for without both, I would not be where I am today. Firmly grounded in Christ and blooming wherever God plants me.

I pray that the words which follow, will also help you bloom wherever God plants you.

$\mathscr{G}$OLD BAND

At the age of eighty-five my mother, Mildred Conklin, was faced with a very tough decision. The doctors discovered she had a large aortic aneurism just above her heart. Her choices: Risky open heart surgery or take her chances that it wouldn't rupture. The odds weren't good with either option! My mother said, "I don't have a choice. I'm not done living for my great grandchildren yet." She opted for the surgery and was moved to a larger hospital in Columbus where surgery soon followed.

As Mom was about to go into surgery the nurse told her that she needed to remove her wedding band. Mom said, "No, you can just tape it. It has never been off my finger." The nurse explained that Mom had to remove the band because it would burn her finger if they had to shock her. Mom reluctantly agreed, but told Dad that he had to remove it, because he was the one that put it on her finger sixty-six years ago. So Dad removed the wedding band and gave it to me.

Following a seven hour surgery, Dad was escorted to see Mom in recovery. The rest of us were winding down the hallways to a waiting room. Suddenly Dad and his escort appeared. Dad wanted to put the ring back on Mom's finger, and I still had it in my purse. He put the ring on her finger but it was once again removed due to the swelling in her hands. Three days later, and upon Mom's request, Dad permanently put the wedding band on her finger once again. What a true testament of love and commitment!

The band is worn and tattered. After sixty-six years of marriage the gold is much thinner than that of a small paperclip. It is so fragile and no longer quite round. There is nothing beautiful about it to the eye, but great beauty lies within. It represents hard times, good times, hard work, raising a family and all the trials of life. It is a symbol of their commitment to their marriage vows. Vows which were taken and upheld to the highest standard.

Just as my parents are married and committed to one another, Christ asks the same of us. Many times in the Bible we are referred to as the bride of Christ. He desires a covenant relationship with each of us. One such example can be found in *Hosea 2:19–20 (NASB).*

> *I will betroth you to Me forever;*
> *Yes, I will betroth you to Me in righteousness and in justice,*
> *In lovingkindness and in compassion,*
> *And I will betroth you to Me in faithfulness.*
> *Then you will know the LORD.*

Can you hear God calling you into a love relationship with Him in these verses? Just as the gold band represents commitment to my parents, God asks us to be fully committed to Him. It is a lifetime commitment to walk with Him daily. We will face trials, but when we are devoted to Christ, He will strengthen us.

> *Trust in the LORD and do good. Then you will live safely in the land and prosper. Take delight in the LORD, and he will give you your heart's desires. Commit everything you do to the LORD. Trust him, and he will help you. (Psalms 37:3–5)*

Commitment. It can be a short term commitment, maybe a few days or weeks to complete a task. Like my parents, it can be a sixty-six year, death-till-we-part commitment. But a lifetime, loving relationship with God will be like no other commitment you will ever make. He will lead you and cover you with grace during times of failure. Please make that promise to the Lord today by praying, "Yes Lord, I love you with all my heart, and I trust in You. I will follow wherever you are leading me today and always. Amen." And, oh, the wonderful places He will take you, once you give yourself to Him wholeheartedly.

TEARS

It amazes me how God's Word continually speaks to my heart. He knows exactly what I need to hear and when I need to hear it. During my Bible reading this morning, a verse spoke to me. I have read the passage before, but today it became a verse of great comfort, one which shows a very compassionate God. All of us have been through difficult times in our lives and have shed many tears along the way. I'm sure you have felt comfort and compassion from friends and family during some of your difficulties. But did you realize that Christ can feel your pain and sorrow more than your friends and family?

As I have grown in my Christian walk, I have learned that God set me apart when He formed me in my mother's womb *(Jeremiah 1:5)*. I understand that He has every hair on my head numbered *(Matthew 10:30, Luke 12:7)*. But I never realized God feels my pain and sorrow and collects my tears.

In *John 11:35* it says *"Jesus wept."* This verse shows Christ's compassion and humanness. He felt the same pain Martha, Mary, and the others felt over the death of Lazarus. Jesus was mourning with them. Feeling their pain. But *Psalm 56:8* shows us His compassion in a deeper sense. It says, *"You keep track of all my sorrows. You have collected all **my** tears in your bottle. You have recorded each one in your book"* (emphasis added).

Christ is so compassionate that He keeps track of your every pain and sorrow. Maybe it was a skinned knee as a child. God

4

wiped away your tears even though you didn't understand it at the time. Or maybe you have recently shed tears from the loss of a loved one. God has those tears in a bottle! Maybe you have cried over a broken relationship or a broken friendship. God has felt your pain and recorded your pain in His book. What an amazing, compassionate God!

But in the midst of your sorrow, remember the compassionate God was also called El Shaddai by the Hebrew people. El Shaddai means God Almighty or the God who is sufficient for the needs of His people. Our sorrow is all part of His greater plan for our lives. Your pain today may lead to greater strength tomorrow. So let God catch your tears as you focus on the cross. May you rest in His loving, compassionate arms because El Shaddai holds your future in His hands.

Spoon of Forgiveness

Have you ever had one of those moments in life, where you think maybe you were temporarily possessed by Satan or something? You just wish you could undo everything that just happened in the last thirty minutes of your life. Wouldn't it be great if you could edit your life just like you edit a document? You could highlight the moment, and press delete! Poof—Gone! Unfortunately, life just doesn't work that way.

One of those moments in my life involved a spoon. It seemed to be my weapon of choice this particular day, funny as it may seem. Earlier in the day, a fellow had treated my teenage son very disrespectfully, including accusations and verbal obscenities. Unfortunately, this wasn't the first incident. He was known for treating others in this manner, including my son when he was younger and played little league baseball.

Something just snapped in me that day. It had been a very long week at the county fair and I was exhausted. It was the last night of events. I was setting up a dinner for the buyers at the Junior Fair livestock sale, and I had borrowed a very long handled spoon from a nearby booth to stir lemonade. Every Christian value I was ever taught vanished. I found myself pointing the spoon in the man's face, defending my son's honor! I literally yanked a cell phone out of his hand, to make sure I had his undivided attention. I invaded his space you might say—to make sure he was as intimidated as my son had been earlier in the day.

Due to my mistake, I had to suffer the consequences for my actions. Those consequences were missing my other son Ryan receive an award for his outstanding work in 4-H. You see, apparently you shouldn't point spoons at people who might call the sheriff. No, I'm not a convicted felon, but I did miss the ceremony due to the sheriff's need to question me. I had actually been accused of hitting the man with a spoon, which was untrue.

So why did I react in this manner, rather than having a stern Christian conversation with him? The first thing that comes to my mind is that I didn't pray first. I was simply an upset mother on a mission to defend her son. I should have been a Christian mother, taking her petition to God. *Philippians 4:6* says, *"Don't worry about anything; instead pray about everything. Tell God what you need, and thank him for all he has done."* I should have been counting my blessings, and asking God for the guidance to handle the situation at hand, and not handling it myself.

Fortunately, God does forgive our sins and *Luke 24:47* says, *"There is forgiveness of sins for all who repent."* But God actually commands us to do even more, in *Matthew 5:44*, Jesus commands us to *"Love our enemies and pray for those who persecute you."* I have learned that one's unconfessed sin can make for a very bitter and ungrateful heart, but confession and forgiveness creates a clean and thankful heart. A heart which is able to be molded into a servant for Christ.

Points to Ponder

- What incident from your past, do you wish you could highlight and delete?
- Have you either forgiven or apologized to those involved? Remember to pray for those involved as well.
- Have you sought God's forgiveness and asked Him for a clean and thankful heart?

HERMOSTAT

Several years ago my son Matt went on a mission trip to Venezuela through the college he was attending. While he was there, part of his work included physical labor in unbearable heat. This past year, my brother-in-law Bumpy went on a mission trip to Honduras and experienced similar conditions. He was loading wheelbarrows with gravel in temperatures between 120–130 degrees. Having come from Ohio where the summer highs are between 90–100 degrees, you could say they were feeling the heat. Matt says, "It brings a whole new definition to the word thirst."

When the two of them were comparing notes, Matt recalled exactly how he felt. He remembers saying to God, "You called me to do your work and I'm giving it my best shot. Couldn't you work with me a little and at least turn down the thermostat?"

Though I can't relate to the heat exhaustion they were feeling, I can relate to the comment. There have been many times in my life when God turned up the thermostat just a little too high! The most recent example happened just this week. In the past few months I have committed to write a devotional book. I also committed to being the Lay Director for the Walk to Emmaus in May for our Emmaus community. Both tasks will be stretching, detail oriented, full of Bible study, growth and prayer. But sometimes along with the personal growth there are trials and circumstances which are out of our control. Problems which make us question God but ultimately build our strength.

Saturday our tractor and a piece of farm equipment were being transported down a state route from one field to another. It suddenly started leaking oil and the check engine light came on. Unfortunately the driver Stan was on a stretch of road with hills and curves and there was nowhere to pull over. You just don't park a tractor and equipment on the shoulder of the road. As he continued looking for an opportunity to pull off, he lost all steering control of the tractor, and was just along for the ride. He slowed the tractor down, rode it through the ditch between two poles and a road sign. The equipment was off the road only by inches when he came to a stop. Blessings—oh yes! Most important, no one was hurt. In addition, the equipment he was pulling was not damaged in the process and nothing was rolled over on the uncontrollable ride through the ditch.

Later that evening, I found myself thinking thoughts similar to Matt's from so many years ago. "You called me to do your work and I'm giving it my best shot. Couldn't you work with me a little and at least turn down the thermostat?" First of all, who knows what the expenses will be to fix the tractor. Second, my husband is away on vacation and I don't want to call and give him the bad news! He works so hard and he deserves at least a few days of enjoyment. I was quickly reminded of a very common scripture.

> *Not only so, but we also glory in our sufferings, because we know that suffering produces perseverance; perseverance, character; and character, hope. And hope does not put us to shame, because God's love has been poured out into our hearts through the Holy Spirit, who has been given to us. (Romans 5:3–5 NIV)*

As if reading these verses wasn't reminder enough that God is in control, I also remembered the talk I would be giving during the Walk to Emmaus. The title is "Perseverance."

Our family persevered through the heat in South America. I persevered through the weekend and withheld the information from my husband so he could enjoy a few days of relaxation before bearing the news. My husband and I will persevere through any expenses we may endure to repair the tractor. I'm sure this won't be the last trial in our lives, but together with God's help we will persevere through it all. It's funny how God can turn up the thermostat to build our character, our hope and strengthen our relationship with Him.

So when life turns up the thermostat and you lose your steering, just persevere.

FURNITURE MOVING

My son Ryan, and his girlfriend, Kim, came to help me move the living room furniture today. It is such a chore but my family grins and bears it about twice a year to please me. I like change but just cannot handle the job myself. We have a very large room, so a couple of years ago we purchased a large L-shaped sofa. I love the sofa, but sometimes it just seems like such a burden. I can't move it by myself and it has to have just the right spot.

A couple of times my sons have moved the sofa across the room, we discovered it didn't fit, and they moved it back again. So Ryan had a brilliant idea to make paper furniture. So I drew the room on graph paper and made paper furniture. Everything was exactly to scale. This will be great! I will design the layout, call them when I'm ready, and it will be a quick easy move. Everyone will be elated that they won't have to move the furniture more than once. Wrong! It didn't work. What looked good on paper just didn't work in the room. Oh it all fit, but I really didn't want to get a running start in the kitchen, hurdling over the back of the sofa to get into the living room. So we painstakingly moved paper furniture around on the graph paper. Much to my dismay, we returned the furniture to the exact location it was six months ago.

After two years of this battle, I have come to the conclusion that there are only two layouts for the room. The summer view and the winter view. In both scenarios the L-shaped sofa must be placed first, then everything else will fall into place. It is large and it is the most important piece of furniture. (Of course my husband would disagree and say his recliner is the most important. As it must also have the correct viewing angle of the TV, with the remote by his side.)

God is our L-shaped sofa. He is large and important and when we put Him first in our lives, everything else falls into place. I love the saying, "God first, family second and everything else will fall into place." But we live in such a busy world that it is difficult to keep our lives in a proper balance. There are times when I struggle with balance. It doesn't take too many frustrating, busy days in a row for me to realize that I have allowed my life to get out of order once again. When I take time to reevaluate, and refocus on Christ, and put Him back in first place, life goes much better.

In *Genesis 20:1–3*, God commands us to have no other gods before Him. When we allow our lives to get out of order, all the stuff becomes another god. Working long hours—to earn more money, to purchase more luxuries, can become more important than time with God. Spending more time at the ballpark, or watching football on television, can become more important than time with God. Serving on one more church committee can become more important than time with God. When we don't put Christ first in our lives, any other activity can become a god we worship. There are so many opportunities and activities available that it is hard to live a balanced life. We need to make wise choices in our lives which will glorify Christ, allow us to serve, yet still place Him first.

In *2 Corinthians 9:8* we are told, *"And God will generously provide all you need. Then you will always have everything you need and plenty left over to share with others."* In other words, when we put God first in our lives, we will have more time for family and friends, more money, more blessings, more and more of all we could ever ask for.

Where is God in your life? Is He number one? Take some time today to evaluate your priorities and see what adjustments you might need to make. Start by praying and ask God to help you adjust your priorities so you can make Him first in your life. God is patiently waiting. Will you make Him number one today?

CORN AND RAIN

Once again this year, farming proves to be a year of great faith. All of the crops were in the ground and struggling to sprout and grow as we headed into a hot dry spell in late May. Corn was planted in the field which surrounds our house. It was so hard to drive in and out noticing the corn curling in the heat. I truly felt like God was turning up the heat to test our faith. My husband had been busy putting extra fertilizer on the corn for days, and had decided to stop until rain was in the forecast. We were truly experiencing weather typical of a hot dry August in late May. Jim was very concerned because he had seen this weather pattern before with the drought on 1988.

Memorial Day came and went and the heat continued. There were several days that week where rain was predicted, but none came our direction. Once again we held onto another prediction of rain on Tuesday night. I awoke to the sound of rain on the sky lights early Tuesday morning, but Jim said it was about over, and we did not have enough rain to help. To our surprise another front moved in that morning and the rain continued to come down. We were blessed with over an inch of rain! When I returned home from work, it looked like the corn had grown two inches that day and continued to grow all week. The soil had been moistened and allowed the corn roots to grow even deeper.

If you look at the design of a corn stalk you will notice how the leaves form sort of a funnel. Any rain that hits the inner part of the leaf is funneled straight down the stalk toward the roots.

As Christians we need to be funnels in our own lives. We need to allow God's love to funnel through us, helping us to bloom where He plants us, growing deeper roots of faith. We had faith that God would send us the much needed rain, but we also had faith that if the rain didn't come, God would provide. Knowing that God heard our prayers strengthens me. He is the Provider for all our needs.

> *When I think of all this, I fall to my knees and pray to the Father, the Creator of everything in heaven and on earth. I pray that from his glorious, unlimited resources he will empower you with inner strength through his Spirit. Then Christ will make his home in your hearts as you trust in him. Your roots will grow down into God's love and keep you strong. And may you have the power to understand, as all God's people should, how wide, how long, how high, and how deep his love is. May you experience the love of Christ, though it is too great to understand fully. Then you will be made complete with all the fullness of life and power that comes from God. (Ephesians 3:14–19)*

God loves us and wants to provide for us. As farmers we experienced a drought and we put our faith in God to see us through. As believers in Christ, we can experience that same drought in our faith during times of trouble. In order for us to walk through those difficult times, we have to plant our roots deep in Christ. Continually reading God's Word, praying and focusing on all He has done for us, helps us to grow during the droughts in our lives. Christ makes our stalks stronger and grows our roots deeper through times of testing. If you are experiencing a spiritual drought in your life, soak in the rain of His love and power. Spend time in prayer and allow God to funnel His love to you so your roots grow deeper. God has blessed you with the Holy Spirit, so allow Him to set deep roots of faith during the droughts of your life.

CAN A MOTHER RESIGN?

As a mother you always feel the pain of your children. Since my children are adults now, can I resign as a mother? Because when they are hurting, so am I. No one told me it would be a lifetime job! Tonight, my married son Matt called from Illinois. He's been out of town on business for over a week. He isn't enjoying his work there, and his newlywed wife is home alone. I could feel his pain, lend an ear, but the only advice and consoling words I had to offer him was that he would be home soon.

Later his brother, Ryan, calls very upset. He just broke up with his girlfriend whom he had dated for over a year. I could hear his agony as he was seeking my advice. Of course he wonders if he made the right decision, and all I could say was, "Only you know if you love her."

As I lie in bed awake at midnight (which is way past my bedtime), my first thought is that they are probably both asleep, and here I am awake worrying about them! I just want to resign as a mother and get some rest. Instead, I focus my thoughts on them and begin to pray. I pray Matt will arrive home safely tomorrow and that his wife greets him with open arms. I pray for Ryan to get some rest as he questions life. I ask God to give him the assurance that He is in control of the outcome, and if the relationship is meant to be, they will overcome their difficulties. I pray that Ryan will seek God's will and guidance as he makes major decisions in his life.

Yet I wonder—does God feel their pain? Does He feel my pain as a mother? Because when they are hurting, I am hurting. I thought of Mary and the pain she must have felt as Jesus hung on the cross! *John 19:25* tells us that Mary stood at the foot of the cross. Can you imagine watching your son suffer on the cross for everyone's sins? She had to see and feel Jesus' agony, yet she stood by Him with no regard to her own heartache.

I realize just how privileged I am as a mother to be able to pray for my sons. Yes, I hurt when they are hurting, but God gave me the honor of being their Mom. Sometimes motherhood is painful, but the rewards far exceed the pangs of childbirth, or the pain of watching them grow into young adults. These verses help me realize that my sons don't mean to put their pain upon me, but they are looking to me for wisdom and guidance.

> *When she speaks, her words are wise, and she gives instructions with kindness. She carefully watches everything in her household and suffers nothing from laziness. Her children stand and bless her. Her husband praises her. (Proverbs 31:26–28)*

What a privilege as a mother! In every situation which arises, I pray God gives me the words of wisdom they are seeking.

On second thought, I don't think I want to resign from motherhood after all. I would rather continue to pray for them. God has given me the best gift of all—two sons who seek my advice and comfort in times of trouble. What a blessing from God to be called Mom.

By the way, it was a short night as Ryan woke me at 6:00 AM to say he made a huge mistake breaking up because she is the best thing that ever happened to him. To which I replied, "Go beg for forgiveness." And he was out the door!

PEELING THE LAYERS

When I was a kid I loved to help my mother peel the wallpaper from the walls. It was fun in that old house to see how many layers you could find. Or even what the layer below looked like. Many times the walls underneath were cracked and we were surprised at all the problems we found. On occasion, Mom had to call in a professional to repair the walls. But other times, the layer below was prettier than the one on top and we wondered why someone would have covered such beauty. The best part of the project was always the end result, a room which was clean and renewed with beauty.

Wallpaper layers remind me of the layers of our lives. Good and bad childhood memories, followed by the painful teenage years. Marriage or maybe the lack of a marriage. Possibly even the loss of a loved one or parent. And of course life can be topped with hurtful words from a friend, possibly the loss of a job or a divorce. We face so many trials in a lifetime, but how we face these challenges can be the difference between the layers we hide behind, and the layers we peel off.

To me, God is my Professional. No matter what the trial is in my life, He shows up just when I need Him. He fills the cracks in my broken life! When I was struggling following my divorce, He set my feet back on His path. He gave me strength to be a single parent and to start each day knowing of His forgiveness and grace.

More importantly, God peels off my layers of shame, hurt, shyness and bitterness. I love to carry around all my layers. They feel like a safe haven I can hide behind. But the truth is, they are ugly! Once I let God peel off these layers, I find myself, the person God designed me to be. So many times when Christ peels off our layers, He finds beautiful hidden talents, which we have buried behind years of cover up and lack of confidence.

In *John 8:1–11*, we read about the Pharisees bringing a woman who was caught in adultery before Jesus. They wanted to stone her, as was the custom in the Law of Moses, but Jesus started to peel off the Pharisees layers and hers! He asked who among them was without sin. The Pharisees realized that none of them could cast the first stone, as they were all guilty of sin. I like to think that the Pharisees had a moment of guilty conscious, as they slowly walked away.

But let's focus on the layers of guilt and shame from the woman. She had lived a very sinful life, but she realized that God had forgiven her. She acknowledged Jesus as Lord. She realized Jesus saved her life and her spirit! God doesn't tell her to go hide behind her layers of the past. In verse *11* He says. *"Go and sin no more."* He peeled off her layers with forgiveness.

My prayer for you today is that you allow Christ peel off the layers of your life. It will feel so good to see the beauty underneath as you make Him the Lord of your life.

Points to Ponder

- Read *John 8:1–11*.
- What layers of your life do you need to allow God to peel off?
- What unconfessed sin might be keeping you from letting your light shine for Christ?

REATER LOVE

*Greater love has no one than this: to lay
down one's life for one's friends.*
John 15:13 (NIV)

If you look at this verse in context, it sounds as if we are actually supposed to die for our friends. There is no doubt in my mind that there are cases where this would actually happen. A mother or father might die to protect one another or their children from harm. But I have recently had an example of this verse which has touched my heart dearly.

My son Matt and his wife, Gina, have put their lives on hold these past few weeks. Gina has encountered problems with her pregnancy which has required her to have limited duty for the remainder of the term. Gina is truly an example of one "laying down their life" for the sake of her unborn child. She had to put her teaching career on hold six weeks earlier than planned. If the pregnancy had gone as planned, she would have missed very few days in the school year. In addition, her social calendar is on hold, as she spends many hours home alone resting. There is no shopping, no cooking, and no cleaning. (Maybe this isn't really a sacrifice, but a blessing though.) There is however lots of boredom, books and TV. The one that touches my heart deeply is that for the sake of the baby, she has refused any medication for the contractions she is experiencing. Not every moment is difficult, but there have been some rough moments, yet she endures. There have been many restless hours as she wonders if this is real labor or just another contraction.

Matt has also "laid down his life" during these few weeks. He recently accepted a promotion at his job, which requires more travel. But he has stayed by Gina's side. He has used phone conferencing to stay in touch instead of attending meetings. In spite of working a job and helping on the family farm, he has become Mr. Mom and has taken over the shopping, cooking and cleaning. This is a very busy time on the farm, but his number one priority has become Gina and the baby. All of this has been a sacrifice for both of them, yet a labor of love for the child which they will soon be holding in their loving arms.

As a result of their example, I think of the little things which we do for others, that makes this verse more tangible. Recently, a friend came to sing at my church on short notice because the gentleman who was coming had a family emergency. That was a sacrifice of time on her part for the glory of God. Yet she thanked me for the opportunity to serve Christ with her music. I often sacrifice my time to take a meal to someone who is ill. Maybe you have sacrificed your time to teach children, or lead a small group Bible study. There are many opportunities each day for us to "lay down our lives for our friends." Christ truly laid down His life on the cross as a sacrifice for our sins. But during Jesus' three years of ministry, He gave us even greater examples of laying down His life for others through healing, service, teaching, and loving others.

How about you? What will you do today to spread the love of Christ to others? Is it time for you to lay down your life for a friend today?

ESUS WEPT

For years when someone would mention memorizing a Bible verse, I would quickly quote *John 11:35, "Jesus wept."* And to be brutally honest, I didn't even know the reference, only the verse itself. It was my way of joking that it was the easiest verse to memorize, or maybe the fact that I didn't really want to memorize scripture at all. But I have come to realize that this small verse in the Bible reveals so much about Jesus.

When you look at the entire story taking place, there is so much revealed about Christ's emotions. Look back at verse *33* it says, *"A deep anger welled up within him, and he was deeply troubled."* Why was he angry? Maybe it was because of their disbelief that Lazarus would be raised from the dead or their frustration that He hadn't arrived sooner. How could His emotions change from anger to tears so quickly? As women, we can easily do the same and to me this shows a compassionate Savior. One who was able to go from anger to empathy in a matter of seconds. When Christ saw their sorrow, He tossed aside His anger and immediately showed empathy for them by crying along with them. This shows us a Savior who is more compassionate than we can possibly understand at times.

Let's fast forward in the story. In verse *43*, Jesus tells them to move the stone and He says, *"Lazarus, come out!"* Lazarus appears! This is his greatest miracle ever performed. I have to wonder if part of the reason Christ wept was because He knew what was about to happen. Sometimes as women we show our emotions more easily than men do, but I have to believe that this was an emotional moment for Christ. The fact that He knew this miracle was about to happen had to stir emotion within Him.

As you continue to read in the gospel of John, no other miracles are recorded after this time. Is it possible that this was the last miracle and that Christ knew it was going to be His last miracle? Could He have been thinking of the agony which was ahead of Him when He felt the anger and then wept? Maybe His tears were actually brought on by fear of the future.

Fear of the future is something I struggle with from time to time. I'm constantly asking, "What's next Lord?" The unknown worries me, yet deep down, I know He is in control of my life. Christ knew the agony ahead of Him was for our salvation. Maybe His tears were actually tears of compassion for each and every one of us.

My thoughts about the easiest Bible verse to memorize have changed drastically when I considered the big picture of the event. For me, it has become one of the most important verses in the Bible. This verse and the story surrounding it show me a Savior who understands all of my emotions. When I read *"Jesus wept,"* it means more than tears to me. It is a verse which says that Jesus cares so much for me, that He is willing to cry with me and to die for me. It is a verse which tells me to be open and honest with Him about all my feelings. My feelings of anger, sorrow, confusion and worry are all important to Him, and He understands. What about you? Have you been honest with Christ about all your feelings today? Come to Jesus today. He is waiting on you.

$\mathcal{F}$LIGHT 93

My husband and I stopped in Shanksville, Pennsylvania this summer on our way home from vacation. This isn't your typical vacation spot, but our son had encouraged us to stop and see the temporary memorial site from Flight 93, which crashed during the attacks on September 11, 2001.

I have to admit my initial response was a little mixed. There didn't appear to be a lot to see, sort of an open field and a few signs posted along a chain link fence. There were some gifts, poems, and letters from visitors propped up against the fence. I heard a lady explaining how there were thousands of such items in storage from visitors over the years and some of it would be displayed once the permanent memorial building was erected.

There was a temporary building on the site which was serving as the museum and an information center. There were several signs around the building which walked us through some of the events of that horrible day. I noticed there were some notebooks along the wall which others were reading. Jim and I joined in and the words we read were heart breaking.

One of the notebooks contained a list of phone calls which were made from Flight 93. No conversations were listed, but it showed the connections they made or who they were trying to contact. Many of the hostages called loved ones. I can only imagine the conversations which would have taken place. Other people tried to call loved ones at several different phone numbers, but never received an answer.

The calls which truly broke my heart were the calls that indicated the line was still open at the time of the crash. I cannot imagine speaking to a loved one in the middle of a hijacking, and then being able to hear the conversations, the commotion and ultimately the crash of the plane. My heart just ached for the friends and families of these victims.

Another notebook contained typed transcripts from the flight recorder. Those were also very difficult to read as you began to understand exactly when the hijackers overtook the jet and the events which followed. Each and every time they were victorious, including the crash of the plane, they were praising Allah.

We left the building much more somber than when we entered. I was holding back tears from all I had read about the horrible disaster. Then God blessed us with such a peace just before we started to pull away. Shortly after Jim started our vehicle, the radio station played, "Jesus Loves Me" by Alabama. To me it was just God's way of saying that He loved the heroes of Flight 93.

I don't know how many of the passengers and crew knew Christ as their Savior, or how many cried out to Him in those final moments before they crashed. I do know that God feels the pain of the loved ones left behind. Some of those loved ones never had the opportunity to say goodbye on that fateful day, while others listened to the horrible disaster from afar and could do nothing but pray.

I also know that life is short and we never know when Christ plans to call us home, or what the circumstances will be. I pray that I remember to show and tell my friends and family how much I love them on a continual basis. I also pray that God will use me to reach the unsaved. I hope all those heroes from September 11, 2001 were able to see God's Light in those final moments.

This is the message we have heard from Him and announce to you, that God is Light, and in Him there is no darkness at all.
1 John 1:5 (NASB)

For God so loved the world, that He gave His only begotten Son, that whoever believes in Him shall not perish, but have eternal life.
John 3:16 (NASB)

WOMAN AFTER GOD'S OWN HEART

Just before going to sleep I read *2 Samuel 2:1*.

> *After this, David asked the Lord, "Should I move*
> *back to one of the towns of Judah?"*
> *"Yes," the Lord replied.*
> *Then David asked, "Which town should I go to?"*
> *"To Hebron," the Lord answered.*

I immediately reread the scripture to my husband, Jim, and asked, "Why was it so easy for David to talk to God and get an answer and it is so difficult for me?" His reply was a little chuckle and he rolled over and drifted off to sleep. There are times when I struggle to hear God speak to me in my spirit, yet it seems so easy for King David. He was described as a man after God's own heart (*1 Samuel 13:14*). Oh to be so close to God that you hear His every word just like David!

I thought about this verse over the next few days. Suddenly, the verse began to convict me about how I had been slowly drifting away from God. My family has walked through some difficult times over the past few months. I did a lot of praying throughout it all—until recently. In the midst of a family disagreement, Jim said "I know you have been praying about this situation and for your sister. What is God telling you?" Those words cut to my soul when I replied, "I haven't been praying." I thank Jim and God for the conviction to get closer to Christ once more. Was it my busy schedule that kept me from praying? Was it because God wasn't answering my prayers with a resounding YES? Or was I just not a woman after God's own heart?

Honestly, I think it is a little bit of all three. We all struggle with busy schedules, and without realizing it we aren't spending quality time with God. We need to always make it a priority to spend time with the Father. We read in *Mark 1:35 (NASB)* where Jesus set that example for us. *"In the early morning, while it was still dark, Jesus got up, left the house, and went away to a secluded place, and was praying there."*

If I am honest with myself, I don't feel like God is answering my prayers to heal my sister Linda who has been seriously ill for months. The pain of this reality has caused me to stop praying, which is wrong of me! More than ever, she needs my prayers for God's will to be done! I am praying for a healing, but I need to accept that God's healing may be to call her home. She would no longer be weak and in pain and she would be reunited with loved ones. As it says in *Job 37:5 (NIV)*, *"He does great things beyond our understanding."* I don't understand why this is happening to Linda, but I can accept it as part of God's plan. In her book, *The Storm Inside*, Sheila Walsh writes, "Jesus calls upon us to follow Him even when we don't understand Him[a]." These words are so true and comforting.

Because of my busy schedule and poor priorities, mixed with discouragement over my sister's illness, I feel like I am no longer a woman after God's own heart. I do believe that Christ feels my pain and I am covered by His grace, which allows me to turn back to Him for forgiveness.

Even though David was a man after God's own heart, he struggled and stumbled from time to time. What set him apart from others was that he always returned to God with a repentant heart and sought forgiveness. God chose David to accomplish many great things. From fighting Goliath to becoming a King. I can't write this devotion and say I understand the ways of God, but I can ask God for forgiveness. This forgiveness will allow me to focus on becoming a woman after God's own heart once again. Just like David was chosen, God has chosen me to touch the hearts of those I encounter, to write devotions and seek Him through the good and the bad.

$\mathcal{D}$ROUGHT INDEX

Unfortunately we are experiencing high temperatures and a moderate drought in Central Ohio this year. My personal opinion is that some fields in the area have a severe drought as the corn appears to be shriveling and starting to die in early July. Since farming is our livelihood, God is definitely testing our faith and our drought index this year. When times get tough, how is your drought index? Do you have scriptures which give you peace in times of trouble?

Due to lack of rain and high heat, I have watered the flower pots on the front porch almost daily. In spite of the high temperatures, they are the prettiest petunias I have ever grown! Several days passed and I forgot to water them. I was just sure they would be wilted, but much to my surprise they were still beautiful that evening. As I poured on a jug of water, I thought, "They must have deep roots to withstand this heat and drought for days. There is no way the soil on top has any moisture for the plants."

That same week, I attended a local church for their prayer hour. The pastor asked for specific prayer concerns. I expressed my concern over the drought situation, and a fear that there would be little or no crop to harvest this fall. Others in the group also expressed various concerns and we prayed specifically for each person's needs. As we closed our time together a lady by the name of Marge, whom I had never met before, asked if she could read a scripture to me. She shared the following with the group.

> *Even though the fig trees have no blossoms,*
> *and there are no grapes on the vines;*
> *even though the olive crop fails,*
> *and the fields lie empty and barren;*
> *even though the flocks die in the fields,*
> *and the cattle barns are empty,*
> *yet I will rejoice in the LORD!*
> *I will be joyful in the God of my salvation!*
> *The Sovereign LORD is my strength!*
> *He makes me as surefooted as a deer,*
> *able to tread upon the heights.*
> *Habakkuk 3:17–19*

After sharing these words of hope with me, she also shared that she too was a farm wife. She had experienced a drought before and these words gave her hope and strength. I was so blessed by these words in Habakkuk that I read them many times this past week. I came home and shared them with my husband, who in turn shared them with other farmers. I now have such a peace as I focus on God, rather than focusing on the drought. I guess you could say it lowered my drought index.

To me the key word in this scripture is **yet**. *"Yet I will rejoice in the Lord!"* In other words, bad things may happen, tough times may lie ahead, but I will still have joy in the Lord. Nothing or no one can take that joy away from me. No one can steal my salvation or keep me from crying on Christ's shoulder. No matter what lies ahead I can rejoice in all He has done for me. I have the security of knowing that God is with me at all times. This wasn't the first time that the drought index was turned up in my life, nor will it be the last. Yet in spite of the high temperatures I have my roots planted deep in the soil of God's Word, just like the petunias have deep roots in the soil. And because of my deep roots, I will rejoice in the Lord always.

HIGH SEAS EXPEDITION

Next week is Vacation Bible School at our church, which means the church is buzzing with people setting up decorations. Some are building a lighthouse, which is a key prop in the sanctuary. Another crew is hanging fish nets and placing old treasure chests around in various places. Signs are going up with sayings such as: "Ahoy matey" "Aye, Aye, Cap'n". Slowly they are transforming the church into the theme of "High Seas Expedition". The teams of people working want to portray a fun, inviting atmosphere for the children who will attend the VBS. Their goal is to create an exciting, learning environment for the children to hear God's Word. But my question is, "Where are they sailing to?" If the kids are going to have this much fun, maybe I want to join them!

I'm sure some people think all the decorations aren't necessary. They might feel it is too much work for just one week of Bible stories. But what if—during that one week of Bible stories, there is one wave of knowledge, in one child's life, which will transform one child's future. Isn't all the effort worthwhile? Won't that child desire to return next week, or next year to learn more about Jesus when he or she has a good time?

I think the same philosophy holds true for us as adults. What if you spend ten minutes each day for one week in God's Word where a wave of knowledge transforms your future? Isn't all the effort worthwhile? Wouldn't you want to return to God's Word for more next week? One little morsel of knowledge can change how you see your future or help you see God's will for your life. Maybe a Bible verse which you memorize this week will help you handle a difficult situation next week. It might give you the wisdom to help a friend who doubts God, or one who is sailing some rough seas.

> *Do not conform any longer to the pattern of this world, but be transformed by the renewing of your mind. Then you will be able to test and approve what God's will is—his good, pleasing and perfect will. (Romans 12:2 NIV)*

When we as Christians take the time to dig into God's Word, we are renewing our minds and allowing God to help us grow. As we grow closer to God, the more we will see Him in the small beauties of life. Like seeing the ocean waves for the first time, or a sunset on the beach. When we see God in the small things, we will find it easier to see God in the bigger picture. Just like a lighthouse on the shore during a raging storm, God is there to guide us through the storms of life. The more we are grounded in Christ, the easier the waves of life become.

We need to stay so close to God that we can set sail on a calm day and know our ship will not capsize when the waves of life suddenly turn into high seas. We want to know God is with us riding each and every wave which comes our way. We need to allow Him to transform our lives, just as the VBS crew transformed the church into a "High Seas Expedition." Let's pray we are able to keep our ship headed toward the Lighthouse each and every day. Together with Christ we will enjoy the smooth sailing days. On the stormy days, our faith and knowledge will sustain us and He will guide us toward the lighthouse where we can safely come ashore.

Lighthouse from VBS

OBJECT OR PERSON

I worked in the animal industry for over twenty years. Within the company, they have numerous ways to identify the animal. There is a number within the company which is unique to each animal. Within the world, there is a different number to identify the same animal. But the workers in the barns working with the animals call them by name. They have a relationship with them.

It is the same with us as human beings. We have social security numbers, driver's license numbers, credit card numbers, and insurance numbers. Numbers, numbers, numbers. Each one identifies us within someone's company. When you call customer service, the first piece of identification requested is your number. We sometimes feel much more like an object, than a person.

Fortunately within our families and friends, we have a name and possibly a special nickname. Maybe you have a nickname such as Honey, Sweet Pea, or Dear. These are loving names, affirming ones affections. Sometimes when I'm correcting my children, I use their full name. This is a different form of affection, but still meant in a loving way. We as parents tend to use both names to get their attention. We may want to protect our children from harm, teach them manners, or important life skills. We use both names to assure their undivided attention to the important lesson that is about to follow!

Our name is very important to God. In *Exodus 33:17 (NIV)*, He told Moses, *"I am pleased with you and I know you by name."* God knows each one of us by name and has called us for His purpose. Sometimes He has to treat us like children as well, to protect us, teach us and lead us in the right direction. He sends trials and difficulties our way to help us grow into better Christians. He never treats us like an object. He knows everything about us and how much we can bear.

God also has many names, each providing its own special meaning. Names like: Creator when you look at the wonder and beauty in this universe. Shepherd when you feel the need for protection, or Living Water when you are looking for strength. Sometimes He is Healer when you are ill or Savior when you come for forgiveness.

We are never an object to God. In the Bible, He often changed ones name to have more significance. In *Genesis 17:1–5, 15–16 (NIV)* El Shaddai, which is Hebrew for God Almighty, changed Abram and Sarai to Abraham and Sarah, which mean father and mother of many nations. He was called God Almighty, because He was about to make Abraham the father of many nations at the age of ninty-nine! It takes God Almighty to accomplish such a miracle.

One of my favorite names for God is Adonai. The name Adonai is Hebrew for Lord. It signifies ownership or mastership. Not only is He the master of my life, but He gives me the ability to accomplish all He asks of me.

The Bible also tells us that there is power in God's name in *Exodus 9:16 (NIV)*, *"But I have raised you up for this very purpose, that I might show you my power and that my name might be proclaimed in all the earth."* When life takes a turn in the wrong direction, call out to God. Ask for His protection, guidance and strength.

I'm not only grateful that God knows me by name, but also thankful that He is my Adonai and I have power in His name to accomplish great things for His kingdom.

Points to Ponder

- God knows you by name. How does that make you feel?
- Which of His many names are fitting for how you are feeling today?
- Search the scriptures for the different names of God.

GPS Adventure

My husband, Jim, and I were vacationing in South Dakota this year. We decided to have a picnic supper one evening, but we couldn't find a park. So we trusted our electronic GPS device to locate the closest park. We were excited to find there was a park about ten miles away.

We headed down this country road, following our trusty GPS device. It instructed us to turn from the country road onto a dirt road, which isn't uncommon in South Dakota. We were actually excited thinking we would be out away from the busy town and have a peaceful picnic. Next thing we knew, our dirt road turned into a pothole dirt road. Then our instructions were to turn onto what was literally a cow path! (The lane which runs behind our property to the creek was better than this road—if you could even call this a road.) But we continued with my husband giggling and me worrying that we were actually on someone's property. There we were bouncing through the potholes, with cows on the left and cows on the right. But my husband was quick to remind me that open range is very common in the west. He loved the adventure, but I on the other hand was getting more nervous all the time.

According to our GPS, we only had two miles to go when we encountered a tree across the path, oh excuse me, the road. It was at this point and much to Jim's disappointment, we decided to give up. I helped him maneuver around the potholes, and stumps to get turned around and head out of the pasture—or open range as he preferred to call it.

For the rest of our vacation, it really bothered Jim that we didn't know what was beyond the tree! He really wished we could have continued for the last two miles through the pasture. Did we make the right decision to give up, or would we have found a beautiful park or maybe a gorgeous lake? Unfortunately, we will never know.

How many times in our lives do we turn around because the path ahead has become too rough! As a Christian it is so easy to expect the path ahead to be beautiful, comfortable and safe. But sometimes the road ahead is like a dirt path with trees, cows and potholes. God uses these rough paths to stretch us and teach us as we grow into stronger Christians. *Psalms 50:48* reminds us that we need to trust God for all that lies ahead in our lives. *"Trust me in your times of trouble, and I will rescue you, and you will give me glory."*

I hope the next time I hit a rough road in my Christian walk that I won't turn around and take the easy road. I pray I am able to remember the GPS adventure and the feeling of never knowing what was beyond the tree. God has many rewards for those who serve Him. We need to trust His lead and continue along the path of life. God will give us wisdom along the way and rewards in heaven for following Him through the potholes along the dirt road of life.

Points to Ponder

- Do you have potholes in your life which you have been avoiding? Ask God for the wisdom to move forward, rather than turning back.
- Are you easily distracted from your Christian walk when potholes come your way? If so, what can you do to stay focused on Christ and trust Him more?
- Is God calling you to a new adventure? Don't wonder what you might have missed one day, instead follow where He is leading you.

$\mathcal{S}$ILO'S EDGE

As a teenager, I can remember watching my oldest brother, Russell, sit on the edge of the silo which is about fifty feet tall. He would climb to the top, shimmy along the edge to the other side, and sit there as Dad hoisted up the blower pipe from the ground. He and Dad had dairy cattle and they needed to position the pipe so they could fill the silo with silage for the cows. Russell never seemed to have a fear of heights, but to me teetering on the edge would have been fearful. How easily it would have been for him to topple over the edge, and fall one way or the other!

Sometimes we teeter on the edge of life. I have recently been faced with many challenges and decisions concerning my profession. My friend is teetering on an edge, but hers is due to a very bad marriage. Another friend teeters due to horrible news of molestation in her family. We are all asking God, "Why me? Why is this happening to my family?" What has you teetering on the edge of emotions in your life? Is it illness, family conflict, or job stress? What do you do when you find yourself falling over the edge?

I recently found myself doing a nose dive off the edge of my silo! Not being able to handle any more stress in my life, a conflict with a friend sent me spiraling off the silo. I felt like I was spinning slowly to the ground. Fortunately my husband, Christian friends and especially God caught me before I crashed. My husband, and friends helped me to look at the situation from the edge of the silo, instead of the nosedive I was doing. This in turn allowed me to seek God for the necessary healing and answers.

> *Dear brothers and sisters, when troubles come your way, consider it an opportunity for great joy. For you know that when your faith is tested, your endurance has a chance to grow. So let it grow, for when your endurance is fully developed, you will be perfect and complete, needing nothing. If you need wisdom, ask our generous God, and he will give it to you. (James 1:2–5a)*

God gives us many trials in life, but I find over and over again, that none of my trials are wasted. God will one day use the turmoil in my life so I can help someone else in the same situation. After the crisis is over and I can focus on God, I find it a blessing to endure trials, because He has a plan I cannot comprehend. So for today, I will continue to seek healing, follow God's guidance, and trust His plan for my life. There will be more days when I spiral off the edge, but God will catch me in His loving arms so that I may continue to serve my Savior.

I pray you find peace and love in God's arms. May His angels here on earth, known as family and friends reach out to you in your time of need. No matter what has you teetering on the edge of your silo, remember God is always there to catch you before you fall.

Suggested Scripture Reading

- *Psalm 4:18–19*
- *Psalm 34:1–7*
- *2 Corinthians 1:3–11*

$\mathcal{W}$RONG SIDE OF THE BED

I have seen signs in stores which say, "Some days I wake up Grumpy and other days I let him sleep." Today was one of those days when I woke up grumpy. But I was the one grumpy, not my husband! I noticed Jim tried to keep his distance until I left for work and I don't blame him. However, I did apologize and gave him a kiss as I went flying out the door.

I was wondering though, why did I wake up with such an attitude? I'm sure you have had mornings like this yourself. As I drove to work, I tuned off the radio and prayed. I really was not in the mood for praise music and thought maybe God wouldn't mind listening to me grumble for a few minutes. He not only listened as He always does, but He showed me many reasons why I awoke with such an attitude. Maybe you can relate to a couple of them.

First, God reminded me of *Nehemiah 8:10 (NIV), "The joy of the Lord is my strength."* What happened to my joy? I had been so busy over the past several days that I had spent very little time with God. My devotions and prayer had become almost nonexistent. Staying connected to Christ keeps us in His will and brings us joy. This led me to analyze my busy life. I need to make some necessary adjustments and make God a priority in my life once again. When I put Christ first not only will I be walking in His will, but everything else falls into place.

I was also reminded of *1 Corinthians 6:19–20 (NIV), "Do you not know that your body is a temple of the Holy Spirit, who is in you, whom you have received from God? You are not your own; you were bought at a price. Therefore honor God with your body."* I can honestly say that this body is not in very good shape these days! It is time to eat better and exercise more. God is counting on me to be His servant which means I need to be able to do whatever He asks of me.

The last reason I woke up on the wrong side of the bed was stress from my job. I knew what was waiting for me at the office! Rather than facing the challenge with a good attitude and committing everything to the Lord, I chose to grumble. Tomorrow, I'm going to walk in the office saying *Proverbs 16:3 (NIV), "Commit to the LORD whatever you do, and your plans will succeed."* God will not only help me succeed, but He will help me to find joy in the process.

Tomorrow I'm going to remember Devotions + Prayer + Discipline = Joy and Success.

Points to Ponder

- Are you reading your Bible and praying daily?
- Are your priorities in order? God, family, friends, work.
- Do you need to eat right and exercise more?

Mountain Peak

My husband and I found it very important to take our sons on a good vacation every summer when they were younger. Spending a week or two on the road with them, taught us so much about their personalities. One particular vacation we traveled from Ohio to see the west! So you can imagine all we stowed away in the minivan for a family of four.

It was during this vacation we discovered our youngest son had a slight fear of heights. When we arrived at the Pike's Peak entrance, Ryan proclaimed that he didn't want to ride in the van to the top of the mountain. He was about eight years old at the time, and insisted he would be sitting right there on the bench when we came back down! Now we all know that an eight year old boy is not going to sit on a bench for very long no matter how scared he is. We insisted he accompany us up the mountainside and reassured him that he would be safe.

We stopped at numerous points along the road enjoying the scenery and to snap a few photos. We always encouraged Ryan to get out and take a look, but being the strong willed child he was, he insisted it was much safer in the van. But amazingly, when we reached the summit, he jumped out of the van and walked around! Having seen Pike's Peak from a distance, I believe in his eight year old mind, he thought the top of the mountain would truly be a point and we would fall off!

Unfortunately as we traversed back down the mountain we were unable to pull over for Ryan to see the beautiful scenery. Most of the stops were on the other side of the road and for safety reasons we couldn't cross lanes to park. Ryan's fear of the unknown and his preconceived conception that the mountain was a point, had kept him from experiencing the beautiful climb to the summit.

How many times in life have I missed out on God's plan for my life for that same type of fear? A simple fear of the unknown or my preconceived view of what lies ahead can stop me from God's spectacular plan. I have heard myself say many times, "No God, I don't want to speak to the group of ladies. What if they don't like my story?" But I hear God reply in my soul, "But what about the one who does hear your story, and it makes a difference?" God doesn't see the group, He sees the individual whom He has placed in my path where I am to be a witness.

I love this reminder in the Psalms that God has His guiding hand upon our fears.

> *I look up to the mountains; does my strength come from the mountains? No, my strength comes from God, who made heaven, and earth, and mountains. He won't let you stumble, your Guardian God won't fall asleep. (Psalm 121:1–3 MSG)*

I don't always feel I have the strength and courage to accomplish everything God asks of me. But I do need to remember that God gives me the strength and courage I need at just the right moment, and to continue serving Him.

PLANTING AND WATERING

Several years ago we moved from the old farm house into a newer home. Though it was difficult to leave behind many memories of raising our children in that old house, the newer ranch home with the huge family room has been a blessing. One thing I miss from the old homestead are the crocus, tulips and daffodils, which are always plentiful in the spring. I have many flowerbeds at the new home, but none with those first signs of spring. My son now lives at the old house and said to come retrieve whatever flowers I desired. So this fall I was on a mission to transplant the bulbs!

The first step was to dig. I was surprised how easy it was to dig the bulbs. We recently had some rain and with every turn of the shovel bulbs just appeared by the handful. I was having a great time, and had visions of a beautiful spring with our sidewalk lined in flowers. So I dug, and dug, and dug. A couple of days later I had the task of replanting all those bulbs. The soil had hardened once again and it seemed as if the bulbs had multiplied in the box. Planting the bulbs was more work than the digging. I lined the front sidewalk with bulbs. I lined the pine trees in the back yard with bulbs, and there were still bulbs to be planted! My hands were sore, my back ached, but I was determined to plant every single one. I had visions of flowers surrounding our house, but I also had one slight problem. The flower bulbs were all similar in shape and size, so I couldn't tell them apart. The mystery of the flowers won't be revealed until spring. Some bulbs may not grow and the variety, color and size may vary. In the spring the arrangement will definitely be a surprise, as tulips, crocus and daffodils emerge.

Just as I have no idea which bulb I planted, sometimes we have no idea what seeds we are planting in a person's life. Several years ago I was miserable in my current fulltime position. I knew God was calling me down a different path, but I didn't understand why or where. One day, I was honored to do the invocation at a company banquet. A fellow coworker later told me that "I had missed my calling." Charlie could see a passion in me to serve in some form of ministry. A passion I could not see in myself at the time. In the months to come, those words echoed in my mind and soul as God began to open doors. With a somewhat heavy heart I left behind many friends. Friends whom I had worked with for over twenty years. I began a new chapter in my life and accepted a part-time position within our church as an Administrative Assistant. The pastor has taken me under his wing and taught me many skills which have helped me pursue my passion of writing devotions. Charlie planted the seed with his words of encouragement. Pastor Matt watered it with his teaching, but God is harvesting as I publish my book of devotions. In turn I hope this book will plant seeds in you.

> *After all, who is Apollos? Who is Paul? We are only God's servants through whom you believed the Good News. Each of us did the work the Lord gave us. I planted the seed in your hearts, and Apollos watered it, but it was God who made it grow. It's not important who does the planting, or who does the watering. What's important is that God makes the seed grow. (1 Corinthians 3:5–7)*

We encounter people every day of our lives. Sometimes God calls us to plant the bulbs and sometimes He calls us to water them. Not every bulb we plant will be a success but we must continue to do His work. Some of the bulbs I planted this fall will not survive. They may be too shallow to survive the cold winter or too deep to ever see the light. Even as Christians we experience times of discouragement and feel as if Christ is miles away. Encouraging words like Charlie's words to me can make a huge difference in a person's life.

Just as my flowers are a mystery until spring, life can be a mystery as well. Sometimes we may plant encouragement and faith, and never know if someone else will water. Sometimes the soil may be easy to dig and immediately the person grows in Christ. Or the soil may be hard and it requires a lot of labor before you see the changes. Hopefully one day the bloom appears as God helps the person to grow. Regardless of whether we see the results or not, we must be diligent in serving Christ by continuing to plant and water because as the words from *Isaiah 26:3–4 (MSG)* say,

People with their minds set on you,
you keep completely whole,
Steady on their feet,
because they keep at it and don't quit.
Depend on God and keep at it
because in the Lord God you have a sure thing.

Keep up the good work and maybe for today you can plant a bulb of encouragement in a friend or coworker. Tomorrow you might have the privilege of watering a young Christian with prayer. As you plant in the soft soil and the hard soil, enjoy the mystery of God's flower garden. One day there will be beautiful blooms in the lives you touch along the way.

WALK WITH CHRIST

You walk today like a star.
Because God says, "Child you are!"

Walk beside Me where I lead.
I will meet your every need.

Through this journey you were called.
I will be your All in All.

Strength for each situation.
With prayer and supplication.

Lead me through each day I pray.
Bring me rest when down I lay.

Strength will rise with each new morn.
In Your loving arms so warm.

Grace abundance overflows
Never ceasing as I go.

When with You I walk along
Singing ever with a song.

CARS

Let's discuss cars for a moment. Not your typical devotion topic, but I think we can learn a lot from the cars we have driven in our lives.

My first car was a Chevy Vega. It was a hand me down from my sister, a standard shift, but I was proud to have a car I could call my own, even though Dad provided it. One thing Dad always said was it was my responsibility to watch the gas gauge. I was not to call him if I ran out of gas! Now deep down I knew he would rescue me, but it was his way of teaching me responsibility. The car served its purpose, and provided transportation for me as I graduated high school, and commuted to college. To me the Vega symbolized learning and responsibility. Just as a new Christian becomes responsible for their actions while they study the scriptures to learn more about Christ.

Fast forward a few years. I'm married with two children and for the first time in my life I'm driving a new vehicle—a Plymouth Horizon. Not an extravagant car, but new, which was something to be proud of at my age. Unfortunately, pride described this era of my life. I was too proud to need Christ, too proud to admit fault, too proud to need help from anyone else. Life became difficult. I was involved in several wrecks. The first one totaled my Horizon, so we purchased another. Much to my dislike, I had several fender benders in it as well. Out of a total of five or six wrecks, only one was my fault. But I also had developed a mentality that problems in my life were not my fault either. Not as a result of the wrecks, but a result of pride, and putting myself first. At the end of the era I found myself a single mom, and God was very distant from my life. As I look back over my life, I was not heeding the warnings of *Proverbs 16:18, "Pride goes before destruction and haughtiness before a fall."*

My next car will always be one of my favorites. My Dad helped me purchase a bigger used car. It was a Chrysler New Yorker and it talked! It was a great car for a single mother of two. Not only did my car talk to me, but that is when I started talking to God again. It also reminds me of friendships, and their importance. My friend Lois did not judge or criticize, but just reached out to me through this difficult time. We would go to craft bazaars, or for pizza. But there was always one rule, I had to drive. Before the night was over she would open her car door as we neared a stop sign just to hear the car say, "A door is ajar." She would just smile and laugh. She definitely was a bright spot in my life when I needed it the most! She was truly an example of *Proverbs 18:24b, "A real friend sticks closer than a brother."*

Then there was the minivan stage! It seems like most mothers go through this stage of their life, as they rush from one child's event to the next. Even though this stage of my life was busy, I found a new trust in God during this era. Serving in the church became more real, and my prayer life became more important, maybe because I was praying for my boys. This was definitely a growing stage of my life as a Christian. As our boys were growing older, and learning to drive, I was growing and learning to follow Christ all the more. I would often take long walks as my time of silence, and *"Lift up holy hands in prayer, and praise the Lord" (Psalm 134:2).*

Next was my PT Cruiser stage. They were cute little cars yet very roomy. I could whip that little car into a parking place anywhere. This was a transitional stage in my life once again. I was learning that life would be different as the boys left for college. I found myself diving into my work more, and once again spending more time talking to Jesus about my children. But I loved this stage of my life! This is when I put my Mom roll more on the sidelines of life, and really focused on who I was, and what God was calling me to do with my life. I began to truly live by the words of *Proverbs 3:6,* *"Seek his will in all you do, and he will show you which path to take."*

Now I drive a Dodge Charger! Yes, I love it. It allows me to be me. It is the first time in my life that I selected a vehicle that was something I wanted, and not what the family needed. Is that selfish on my part? Maybe. This car illustrates so much to me though. It symbolizes my commitment to Christ as I follow my passions, and dreams to serve the Lord in many ways. It provides transportation to my many activities which I enjoy, and to my job at our church. It portrays the love for my husband with the license plates of "I LOVE JR." To me it is a symbol of a life that has gone full circle. From days when Christ was distant, to today when Christ is very near and real.

Yes, the cars in my life have taught me much, but only because Jesus was constantly with me all these years. From the days of the Vega and learning life responsibilities. Through the crashes with the Horizons and my distant years from Christ. The value of friendship learned through a talking car. The strength found in a minivan during a busy life. Learning that life changes with a PT Cruiser and ultimately feeling loved and on course in my Charger. But now I will be a Grandma soon. Do Grandma's drive Chargers or do I need to purchase an SUV?

How about you? What car are you driving during your current stage of life? I pray no matter what your situation, you will find peace in knowing that God is always with you.

HINA COW

As I was dusting in the office today, my eyes focused on a tiny blue and white china cow on the top shelf of my desk. I "retired" from the company where I had worked for over twenty years. The cow is just one of many mementos which now adorn the top shelf of my desk. The china cow was part of Roger's cow collection. I paused for a few moments and thought about him. Roger was very influential in the dairy cattle industry and the company for which we both worked. Roger passed away many years ago and his wife brought items such as the china cow to the office as gifts for his coworkers.

As I paused to look at the little cow, I wondered if Roger knew Christ. I can't recall any conversations with him about God. I remember conversations about genetics and gardening. He loved to share stories of his travels and his home state of New York. But I honestly can't remember any conversation which gives me a feeling of peace that Roger knew the Lord before he passed away. I have to admit, this really bothered me! I started thinking about how I live my life today. Am I bolder in my faith? Do I share Christ more than I did many years ago?

We all find it easy to talk about Jesus with other believers, but it becomes more difficult outside our Christian circle. My personality isn't the type to walk up to an acquaintance and say, "Can I talk to you about Jesus?" In spite of that there are times when I should be bolder. Yet I do feel that I am a witness to Christ in many ways.

I walk by faith and I have no problem letting others know about the wonderful things God has done for me. I stand strong in the Biblical truths for which I believe, but I am just not a person who will confront boldly. But I also think God made us all different. I'm not using that as an excuse for my lack of boldness, but as an example that we all witness differently. Some believers are going to proclaim the Word of God boldly, and others are going to proclaim it by their actions and how they build relationships.

One of my best friends grew up hearing about Jesus, but professes that Christ is not a part of her life. Life has hurt her over the years and she is very independent—independent to the point that she has no need for Jesus. She often makes comments like, "How can a loving God allow bad things, such as cancer happen to His people?" or "How can God really have time for just me?" She knows where I stand, and I know where she stands. It is the basis of our friendship. In spite of this, we enjoy chatting over lunch and catching up on life. Yet I never give up praying for her and I hope one day she will read one of my stories or see Jesus in me and understand how real He is. If one day she finds herself not so independent, I pray I am there boldly standing in the gap to lend a helping hand in the name of Jesus.

> *And pray for me, too. Ask God to give me the right words so I can boldly explain God's mysterious plan that the Good News is for Jews and Gentiles alike. I am in chains now, still preaching this message as God's ambassador. So pray that I will keep on speaking boldly for him, as I should. (Ephesians 6:19–20)*

I may not boldly preach as Paul did to the church of Ephesus, but I do boldly walk in my faith as a means of witnessing. I truly believe that boldness is more than just speaking out for the Lord. Boldness also includes our actions.

I find it a little ironic that a delicate china cow lead me to question the boldness of my faith. We as Christians need to remember to pray for one another—for the boldness to speak, the boldness to walk a Christian life and the boldness to stand in the gap for others.

PRUNING BUSHES

When the lilac bushes bloomed this spring, they were beautiful and the smell of lilacs filled the air. But after the flowers were gone, the bushes were left with dead blooms and branches sticking here and there which were brown and worthless. What was once a beautiful sight and a wonderful scent had become very ugly, so I took out my hedge trimmers and began to work on them. I collected a pile of branches to discard as I rounded the bushes back into some sort of a shape. After completing the job, I really didn't think the bushes looked much better than before. Now just a couple of weeks later as I gaze out my dining room window, I see new growth appearing in the bushes as they are slowly becoming pretty once again. The trim job was well worth my time and effort because next spring there will be even more beautiful blooms and the scent will be even stronger because the bushes will be healthier.

This reminds me of the very familiar story in *John 15* where Jesus teaches us about the Vine and the branches. Christ is the Vine to which we need to stay connected and we are the branches which unfortunately often need trimmed. If you look at verse *2* it says, *"He cuts off every branch of mine that doesn't produce fruit, and he prunes the branches that do bear fruit so they will produce even more."*

The work I did on the lilac bushes was not a matter of cutting off branches that didn't produce fruit. They would still have produced some blooms next spring, but not as vibrant. I was pruning the branches so they would bear more, vibrant blooms. For a week or two the bushes were not a pretty sight but they have slowly taken form with beautiful, green growth. But that doesn't mean the pruning will not take place again. It is an ongoing cycle to produce growth, which is exactly what God does with us.

Just as I will continue to prune the lilac bushes, God continues to prune our branches to create more beautiful lives. He wants us to become more rounded Christians, ones who produce more growth for His kingdom each day. I believe He prunes in various ways in our lives. Some are simple acts of love, like a friend that wonders in and out of our lives for a short time or a season. While they are a part of our lives they help us grow. Just as my bushes were not a pretty sight after the pruning, pruning in our lives can sometimes be ugly; maybe the loss of a loved one, illness, a divorce or even a wayward child. Even when these things happen to good people, God has a way of trimming our branches to make us better. Though the situation may be ugly at the time, those who are connected to the Vine will eventually grow as a result of the pruning in their lives. After a period of rest and re-growth they become more vibrant, sweet smelling Christians. God never promised that Christian life to be easy, but He has promised to always be with us while He is pruning back the branches.

When God prunes your branches, don't become the dead limb in the trash pile. Allow Him to show you new growth and a new way of life, a life in which Christ sustains you and directs you.

> *Though I am surrounded by troubles, you will protect me...the power of your right hand saves me. The Lord will work out his plans for my life—for your faithful love, O Lord, endures forever. Don't abandon me, for you made me. (Psalm 138:7–8)*

As you walk through one pruning after another in your life, remember to stay focused on the Vine and allow Him to direct your paths to a new, stronger life that thrives.

<u>Suggested Scripture Reading</u>

- *John 15:1–17*

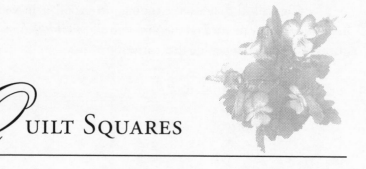

QUILT SQUARES

I like to sew on occasion. Now I'm not a proficient seamstress like other members of my family, but I do like to dabble at it for special occasions. Well this particular project is one of those special occasions because I am making a quilt for my first grandchild! We don't know if they are having a boy or a girl, so I selected denim for one side in case it is a boy and pink flannels on the other side for a girl.

I had spent days cutting up squares of fabric, arranging them in some sense of a pattern and was ready to sew. Well I began to sew, and immediately could tell that my sewing machine was broken! It had been repaired before, and it was just time for a new one. So I purchased a new machine, and started sewing again. But this time the squares just didn't line up correctly. The second row was much longer than the first row, and the third row was somewhere in between. I instantly knew this was not going to work, and in frustration I quit sewing for the day.

My quilt making experience reminds me that if a day is not hemmed in prayer, it just unravels. Some days feel broken just like my sewing machine! No matter what I do, things don't seem to go right. Many times when this happens, I realize that I never took time to pray. I probably didn't pray that morning, I didn't pray when things started going wrong, and I definitely wasn't praying after all the problems occurred!

Yet Paul teaches to pray about everything in *Philippians 4:6.* *"Don't worry about anything; instead, pray about everything. Tell God what you need, and thank him for all he has done."* Pray about everything? Even a quilting problem? Yes, God already knows you are frustrated, so talk to Him, and maybe He will offer you a solution. Praying gives you that inner peace which will help you refocus, and think of ways to solve the problem at hand.

Yesterday I was frustrated, and had no solution on my own. My husband even offered an opinion, and he doesn't sew. I stepped away from the quilting problem yesterday, and today is a new day. I have spent time with God this morning. I feel refreshed, prayed up, and ready to try again. I have a possible solution to fix the problem, and if that doesn't work, I will call on the proficient seamstresses in my family for advice. Yesterday, instead of praying, I was ready to gather up all the pieces, and put them in the trash. It is amazing what a little prayer can do, even for the simple problems of life.

Through making a quilt, and having a few sewing issues, God reminded me that life isn't perfect, but it does go better when it is hemmed in prayer. Take a few moments today to read other scriptures about prayer, and spend a few moments talking to God. He will definitely keep your day from unraveling!

<u>Suggested Scripture Reading</u>

- *Psalm 20:5*
- *Psalm 34:6*
- *Colossians 4:2*
- *1 Thessalonians 5:17*
- *James 5:13*

$\mathcal{B}$ALANCE

Well, today is the dreaded day. I have to balance the checkbook. Most of the time I find that our checkbook balances just fine and it is no big deal. But there is that fear of an error lurking in the numbers. It creates so much work to find the calculation error and correct the problem. Or maybe it is just the word "balance" that bothers me. Balance applies to so many aspects of our lives.

For a child's teeter totter to work, it has to be balanced. For a marriage to work there has to be balance. For an office to function properly, the workload has to be balanced between employees. To maintain a healthy lifestyle there has to be a balance of nutritional foods, relaxation and exercise. For a gymnast to walk a balance beam, she has to have physical balance. As Christians we need to balance Bible study, prayer, meditation and service. Balance, balance, balance! It is everywhere in our lives and sometimes creating balance can make us uncomfortable because it causes us to change or correct a part of our lives.

Our spiritual lives need to be full of checks and balances as well. I consider myself very lucky to have accountability partners. On a regular basis, we ask each other questions like: How is your prayer life and Bible study? How have you served Christ this week? How has your faith struggled this week? But over the years it has grown into a relationship which is much deeper than just these types of questions. Honesty, integrity and trust are at the center of our friendships.

Allowing ourselves to be open and honest with one another, has taught us to also be open and honest with Christ. When we correct each other for our undesirable actions, we find it much easier to ask forgiveness from Christ. We aren't the perfect Christians who make all the correct choices in life. We struggle and stumble just like everyone else. But the difference is when I stumble, they are there to set me back on my feet and vice versa. The teeter totter of our lives might be going back and forth, but we balance one another.

The reason this accountability is so important to me is because I never want my actions to cause another person to stumble. Paul even warns of this in *1 Timothy 4:12, 16 (NIV). "Don't let anyone look down on you because you are young, but set an example for the believers in speech, in life, in love, in faith and in purity. Watch your life and doctrine closely. Persevere in them, because if you do, you will save both yourself and your hearers."*

As a Christian leader in my home, my church and my community, I need to keep balance in my walk with Christ and I cannot do that alone! I'm responsible for my actions, but knowing there are partners who will ask me questions really makes me stop and think about my actions before I take a step.

When I let Christ down through my actions, they have also helped me through these difficulties. Causing another person to stumble in their faith can be very painful. It is like trying to find the calculation problem in your checkbook. It takes so much work to correct. But when you have friends who continually put your feet back on the balance beam of life it is so much easier. Their job is to set me on the right path, remind me to focus on Christ and tell me to just start walking once again. Sure I'm going to stumble, and sure I'm going to fall, but with their help I will always continue to persevere and try to walk a balanced life in Christ.

How is the balance in your spiritual life? Do you need the support of a friend who will continually help you focus back on Christ? If you don't have a partner on the other end of your teeter totter, I would encourage you to find that person in your life that will help you maintain a balanced life in Christ.

OLD FAITHFUL

My husband and I have had the opportunity to vacation in Yellowstone National Park on several occasions. No matter how many times I have seen the sight, I love to watch the Old Faithful Geyser erupt and display its beauty. As it spews steam and water into the air, I am totally in awe of the fact that God created something that is so beautiful. This past trip I was able to record the eruption and I have watched the video numerous times. It is such a powerful sight and one that I truly love. Old Faithful has faithfully erupted approximately every ninety minutes for years. Yet it's faithfulness is nothing compared to the faithfulness of the Creator of such beauty!

Hebrews 11:1 (NIV) tells us, *"Now faith is being sure of what we hope for and certain of what we do not see."* I think faith is an element of my life, which has grown stronger over the years. When I reflect on situations where God was faithful, it helps build a new faith within me. I can recall moments in my life where I was struggling, yet God was there. I didn't see Him at the time, but when I look back, I see His hand was at work in my life through every situation. Through the good and the bad, the happy and sad, the moments of joy and the times of tears. I can truly say that God has always been faithful.

God has faithfully sent me wonderful Christian mentors and friends who keep my feet firmly planted in His Word. God always shows up when I need Him the most. He always leads me when I step out in faith to serve. Most importantly, He is always faithful to listen. I simply need to seek Him in all situations.

God has not only given me an opportunity to serve, but He has also blessed me with the opportunity to work with many of His faithful servants along the way. I am blessed to know this faithful God. He is the one who created Old Faithful as a reminder that He is more powerful and more faithful than any geyser which He created for our enjoyment. He is more than I can fathom or understand, but I know He is always there. To me, God is Old Faithful!

You faithfully answer our prayers with awesome deeds,
O God our savior.
You are the hope of everyone on earth,
even those who sail on distant seas.
You formed the mountains by your power
and armed yourself with mighty strength.
You quieted the raging oceans
with their pounding waves
and silenced the shouting of the nations.
Those who live at the ends of the earth
stand in awe of your wonders.
From where the sun rises to where it sets,
you inspire shouts of joy.
Psalm 65:5–8

Old Faithful Geyser

$\mathcal{S}$OAR LIKE AN EAGLE

Isaiah 40:30–31 (NIV) has always been one of my favorite verses in the Bible. *"Even youths grow tired and weary, and young men stumble and fall; but those who hope in the Lord will renew their strength. They will soar on wings like eagles; they will run and not grow weary, they will walk and not be faint."*

I have always felt such power in these words, yet at times didn't quite understand them. It sounds so simple, if we have hope in the Lord, we won't grow weary. But the truth is you and I do get weary. We live in a busy world. We rise early in the morning, sometimes already weary just thinking of our busy schedules for the day. We all have lists, agendas, and appointments which have to be completed before sunset. I have been there. Haven't we all?

Recently, God has blessed me with the privilege of having a bald eagle nest a short distance from our home. Unfortunately, I seldom get to see them fly. In the spring it is easy to see them sitting on their nest, but being outside at the right time to see them in flight seldom happens.

Saturday was one of those busy spring days. A day where I had hit the ground running, and had not taken time for God that morning. I was outside cleaning trash from the fields and roadside when I noticed the bald eagle soaring above. I stopped and took a few moments to watch him, and realized how effortlessly it was for him to fly. He just seemed to glide higher and higher with such ease.

He didn't have to move his wings he just glided along as if he was soaring toward heaven.

As he soared, I remembered the verse in Isaiah. God gave me such a visual image to explain what it truly means to soar on eagles wings! When we grow tired and weary from life, we need to refocus on God and allow Him to lift us to new heights. When we take time to focus on God, He renews our strength, and gives us hope. When we pause from our busy lives and take time to worship, pray and read the Word, we too will feel as if we are soaring on eagle's wings. God will lift us higher and higher giving us strength for each new day. He will take us to places we have never seen before. Have you taken time to soar with God today? Ask Him to lift you above the clouds of work and worry so you can glide with Him in the warmth of His love and sunlight today.

<u>Tips to Soar</u>

- Keep a Bible or study materials in your vehicle so you can study while waiting in the carpool, or for an appointment.
- As you rise each morning say, "Good morning God." Thank Him for your many blessings.
- Write Bible verses on index cards. Take them along and memorize the verses, when time permits.
- Set aside time each day to pray.
- Find an accountability partner or a Bible study group.

$\mathcal{S}$TEP OF FAITH

I often wonder when I'm taking those little steps of faith, if people really notice. Does my example of Christian faith have an influence on others? For example, a couple of years ago I quit my high stress, high paying, fulltime job to work part-time as an Administrative Assistant for our church. It was definitely a step of faith, yet I felt sure that God was calling me to work at the church. God has provided for us financially every step of the way. I can't always explain why or how this happens, but I have faith that it will continue because I am working where God has called me.

Let's take a look at the scripture of a lady who had the faith to touch the hem of Jesus' robe to be healed.

> *Just then a woman who had suffered for twelve years with constant bleeding came up behind him. She touched the fringe of his robe, for she thought, "If I can just touch his robe, I will be healed." Jesus turned around, and when he saw her he said, "Daughter, be encouraged! Your faith has made you well." And the woman was healed at that moment. (Matthew 9:20–22)*

The scripture says she had been bleeding for years, which means that she was considered unclean by the culture of that day. So she was stepping out in faith just to be among the crowd. She took her faith a step further and touched the hem of Jesus' robe believing she would be healed. This lady showed incredible faith! She not only risked being out among the crowd when she was unclean, but she reached out to Jesus to be healed. She had heard of His miracles, and believed in all that He could do. This simple act of faith set an example for others who would eventually do the same.

Fast forward a few chapters and read *Matthew 14:36, "They begged him to let the sick touch at least the fringe of his robe, and all who touched him were healed."* Wow! Do you think they wanted to touch the hem of His robe because they had heard of the woman's healing? This woman had an unbelievable testimony. The scripture doesn't say that she witnessed to others about her miracle. Maybe she told others, "I simply touched the hem of His coat and Jesus healed me." But maybe she said nothing, and they watched the example she set. Her example of great faith to be among the crowd that day, to reach out to Christ and touch the hem of His garment.

Now I'm not saying that if you are stressed at work you should quit your fulltime job. I am saying that we need to understand that other people watch our steps of faith. There is a very common saying, "Don't just talk the talk, but walk the walk." There is a lot of truth in that statement. I didn't just wake up one day and decide to quit my job. There were many steps involved.

The stress of my current job was taking a toll on me, and I had been praying for quite some time for God's guidance. There was suddenly a notice in the bulletin that they were looking for help, and my son nudged me to apply. I had to secure health insurance for both my husband and me, since he is self- employed. I struggled with the thought of leaving my work family, as many of us had worked together for twenty years. And of course I continued to pray! Through all this time, the church was willing to wait for an answer, and for everything to fall into place. To me this was just another sign that I was making the right decision. As I made my decision, God gave me a great peace about the changes. I haven't worried about our finances, and I have stayed in touch with my old work family, and built new relationships as well.

So the next time God nudges you to step out in faith, think of those who are watching. Start by praying, set a plan into motion, and wait for that inner peace, or signs that you are following God's will for your life. Then slowly take a step of faith. Envision yourself like the woman in the story, reach out and touch the hem of Jesus' robe. You won't regret it, because He will bless you every step of the way.

$\mathcal{M}$YA ANN

Children are a gift from the LORD; they are a reward from him.
Psalm 127:3

This verse has new meaning because I am now a Grandma! It was an exciting day for the entire family. Gina's immediate family was gathered in the waiting room at the hospital. I received word that Jim and I should come quickly, because labor was progressing very rapidly. As is typical fashion, I was in a bigger hurry than Jim. I did not want to miss the opportunity to hear Matt say, "It's a boy!" Or, "It's a girl!" Unlike most parents today, Matt and Gina decided early in the pregnancy to be surprised at the time of delivery. I have to admit, it added a little excitement in the waiting room. Gina's dad recorded everyone as we all guessed the gender and weight of the baby.

Well, Jim and I arrived in plenty of time. Even Uncle Ryan left work early to surprise his brother and be there for the big announcement. Tears filled my eyes as Matt came into the waiting room and announced, "It's a girl, and her name is Mya Ann."

It was a rough pregnancy and an even tougher delivery for Gina, but all were doing well. God had blessed me with two boys in my life, but my first grandbaby is a GIRL! I am excited beyond belief. We were all celebrating a new life and thanking God for the great news that everyone was healthy and doing well. Jim and Ryan brought some BBQ wings and sodas to the waiting room. We had our own little family party, as we anxiously awaited our turn to see Mya for the first time. Everyone was texting and calling friends and family with the good news.

A month has already passed, but I still remember that day as if it was yesterday. Now as I think ahead I wonder, as a Grandma, what is my role in Mya's life? Is my role to spoil her with cookies and ice cream and send her home at the end of the day? Is my roll to babysit her whenever necessary? Do I buy her cute dresses with bows and ribbons? I'm sure I will do those things, but this scripture made me realize my role as Grandma is much more important than cookies, ribbons and bows.

> *Timothy, I thank God for you…I remember your genuine faith, for you share the faith that first filled your grandmother Lois and your mother, Eunice. And I know that same faith continues strong in you. (2 Timothy 1:3, 5)*

Our grandparents influenced the lives of Jim and me. The circle of life continues and our parents influenced the lives of our children. Now it is our turn to do the same for Mya. It is too early to know what Mya will do in her lifetime or even how many grandchildren we may have. Jim and I will make some mistakes along the way, just as we did raising the boys. In spite of this, God will help us be Christian role models who will hopefully influence Mya's life. The simple things like reading her Bible stories and praying before meals will help set a Christian foundation. What a privilege from God to be able to pray for Mya now and as she grows!

It's hard to believe that I am in the grandmother stage of my life, but life marches on. Even though having Mya come into my life helped me focus on the importance of the verses in *2 Timothy*, the lesson goes much deeper than being a grandmother. As part of the body of Christ we are all called to be Christian grandparents. We need to treat others like grandbabies. Pray for one another.

Encourage them. Guide a friend. Share in their blessings and their sorrows. Participate in Bible studies. There are so many ways to reach out to others. If we would all treat one another like we treat our grandchildren, what a wonderful world we would live in! Jesus loved children. And each one of us is a child of God, so let us learn to treat one another with the love deserving of a child as it says in *Mark 10:14b, 16, "'Let the children come to me. Don't stop them! For the Kingdom of God belongs to those who are like these children.' Then he took the children in his arms and placed his hands on their heads and blessed them."*

CLEANSING RAIN

One evening on vacation we rented a cabin at Whitefish, Montana. It was a peaceful setting and I decided to do my daily Bible reading on the porch. In spite of the chill in the air, the sun was shining brightly. My reading for the day was *Ezekiel 45* and *46* and I have to admit it was very hard for me to stay focused on the scriptures. I was surrounded by beautiful scenery, and I was reading about the old law and the sacrifices for atonement.

After reading for some time I wondered, why do I have to read about the ephah, atonement and sacrifices? What is an ephah anyway? Was it two-thirds of an ephah of wheat and one lamb on the New Moons or the Sabbath? Or was it one bull calf and one ephah of barley for atonement? I have to wonder, how did they remember all of this? As I sat praying I asked God, "Why do I care about this stuff from the old law?"

In spite of my lack of interest, I continued to read and meditate. Suddenly out of nowhere, a gentle sprinkle of rain came down in huge drops. Not to be interrupted from my scenery, I moved my chair back under the overhang of the cabin, and quietly watched the rain. As I did so, I felt the Lord answer my question about all this stuff. He spoke to me in my soul, "I want you to understand that I came to cleanse you like the soft gentle rain. You don't have to remember all the rules of the old law, but you do have to understand that I changed all of that for you. I came and died for your sins, so you don't have to follow the old law."

We read of Jesus' crucifixion in *Matthew 27:45–56 (NIV)*. In verse *46* Jesus cries out, *"My God, my God, why have you forsaken me?"* Verses *50–51* go on to tell us, *"And when Jesus had cried out again in a loud voice, he gave up his spirit. At that moment the curtain of the temple was torn in two from top to bottom."* This curtain divided the Most Holy Place from the Holy Place in the temple. The tearing of the curtain symbolizes our ability to talk to God directly, and walk with Jesus personally. What a wonderful feeling that Christ died so we could be cleansed by Him and be filled with the Holy Spirit.

Wow, the thought of Jesus washing away my sins like a soft gentle rain came over me and I tingled from head to toe, as if I had just been baptized once again. As I sat watching the rain, I was absorbed in God's love for me, and He offers that same love to each one of us.

The psalmist David writes in *Psalm 32:5*, *"Finally, I confessed all my sins to you and stopped trying to hide my guilt. I said to myself, 'I will confess my rebellion to the Lord.' And you forgave me. All my guilt is gone."*

To receive this cleansing gentle rain, all we need to do is confess our sins to the Lord. He does all the rest by washing them away. *Proverbs 16:15* tells us that *"When the king smiles, there is life; his favor refreshes like a spring rain."* I know God sent the rain to refresh me that day. As quickly as the rain came, the sun once again reappeared. It was an amazing moment with God.

Today when I open my bible to *Ezekiel 46*, I can see dried spots where the rain drops landed that chilly afternoon in Montana. I pray that they will always serve as a reminder to me that Christ has washed away my sins like a gentle rain. I pray you too will feel the cleansing rain of the Savior and be blessed by the Holy Spirit in your life.

Worker Bee

An unappreciated worker bee—Rejected by peers—
Forgotten at the party—Taken for granted

Have you ever felt like that and then realized you are at church! It is a horrible feeling to "belong to the family of Christ" and still "not belong." I felt all of these while setting up for an event at our church recently. It was a very long day of just feeling like I didn't fit in. No one's actions were intentional, but it made me wonder if I had ever treated others in the same manner. Normally I would brush off an incident like this and move on, but God had a lesson for me to learn.

As I thought over the many emotions, I reflected on the disciples and how they must have felt while establishing the early church. There had to be times when they felt like unappreciated worker bees who were easily taken for granted in spite of all their hard work. They were obviously rejected by some of their peers for following Jesus as well. Yet they continued in the face of adversity. They traveled from town to town and spread the story about the Good News. Starting at *Acts 16:16,* we read about Paul and Silas being severely beaten and thrown into prison for healing a demon possessed girl. As we read on in the story, verse *25* says *"Around midnight, Paul and Silas were praying and singing hymns to God, and the other prisoners were listening."* Singing praises! Are you kidding me! Beaten and imprisoned and they are praising God! But as a result of their faithfulness to God, the jailer and his family were saved and they were released from prison. Now that is reason for praise!

Yes, I was emotionally bruised, but not physically beaten. But I learned that there is healing in praising God because that is exactly what I did. Christian artist, Mandisa, has a song titled, "Broken Hallelujah[b]" on one of her CDs. I found myself listening to her song a couple of times that evening and even singing a "Broken Hallelujah" to the Lord in my mind as I drifted off to sleep. Singing phrases like: "My heart's in a thousand pieces, maybe even more," released me from my mental prison, and opened the door for me to see God's hand in this experience.

As a well grounded Christian, I was hurt by others but I will survive and continue to serve. What about the new Christian trying to find their way in the church? Would he or she return? It is so easy for cliques to form within a church as bonds grow stronger between people. They aren't intentional, but we need to be intentional to include newcomers into the flock. I prayed and asked God for forgiveness if I had ever unknowingly treated someone poorly as a leader or coworker in the church. As a result of my pain, I will grow and remember to reach out to others with appreciation and compassion. Just as Paul and Silas continued to do in their ministry, I too will continue to share the Good News.

The Bible is full of stories of unappreciated worker bees, but the most unappreciated of them all was Christ himself. He was rejected by his peers, the Jewish people. He was spit on by Roman soldiers. He was crowned with thorns and mocked. He died a horrible death on the cross, yet He forgave their sins and ours.

Now I understand why Paul and Silas were able to praise God in prison. Christ suffered so much more than we can ever comprehend. Whether we are singing praises in our pain or praises of joy, Jesus promises us so much more. So yes, I was emotionally bruised, but Christ was wounded far worse, and forgave. This is one worker bee who now appreciates the disciples' perseverance and Christ's forgiveness even more than she did before. And I will continue to sing hallelujah praises until Christ's return because *Revelation 19:6 (NIV)* says, *"Then I heard what sounded like a great multitude, like the roar of rushing waters and like loud peals of thunder, shouting: 'Hallelujah! For our Lord God Almighty reigns.'"*

<u>Suggested Scripture Reading</u>

- *Acts 16:16–40*

THINGS TO DO

Are you a planner and a doer? I had my list of things to do this morning. My list was only in my head, but I was on a mission to accomplish all I could for the day. I needed to dust and vacuum the house, run to the store, take lunch to the men working in the field, finish the laundry, and so forth. But first I need to take a walk. I keep saying I'm going to start exercising and today is the day! After all, I love taking a walk on a brisk autumn day. The crisp air is so refreshing.

I turned out of my driveway at a fast pace. My first leg of the journey took me past some huge pine trees with their wonderful scent. I took several deep breaths and it reminded me of Christmas, and how quickly it is approaching. (Christmas shopping. I need to add that to my things to do list soon.) Walking along the edge of the corn field, I noticed all the ears of corn were turned downward to dry. I thought to myself, "How amazing!" God designed the corn to do exactly what is necessary to dry the kernels for harvest. It looked like all the corn in the field had bowed their heads in reverent prayer. On my return route I walked past the neighbor's property and could see cobwebs glistening in the grass from the morning dew. The sun was peaking in and out of the clouds, just bright enough to make the grass shine. It was too early in the season for fall colors in the trees, yet God let everything else shine today.

I feel so blessed and amazed when I take time to look around at all the beautiful scenery God has given me to enjoy. For today,

He placed the spiders in the grass to build cobwebs just for me. He caused the trees to give off a refreshing scent and the ears of corn to bow their heads in praise. I know God does this each and every day. I am the one who does not stop to see the beauty He creates. I'm too busy with my list of things to do.

During times like these, I feel so blessed and so thankful. God cares so much for me that He created the scenery to refresh me as I walked down the road spending time in prayer and just enjoying my beautiful surroundings. The Bible tells us this in *Romans 1:20*, *"For ever since the world was created, people have seen the earth and sky. Through everything God made, they can clearly see his invisible qualities—his eternal power and divine nature. So they have no excuse for not knowing God."* To know God is more than just loving God, it also means enjoying every moment with Him. From the morning dew to the setting sun, God creates each new day for you and me to enjoy. It is his picture of love for us to embrace. Sometimes it is so hard for me to understand God's omnipotent powers because of my own humanness. I can plan what I would like to accomplish tomorrow, but only God truly knows what the future holds.

We live in a fast paced, busy world. I love planning, and I think God enjoys it when we are thinkers and doers. There are just many times when we need to slow our pace, look around at the beauty He has given us to enjoy and ask God what He has planned for us today. My list of things to do today included a morning walk, but they didn't include writing this devotion. Yet God had other plans for me. I am so glad I was able to feel Him tugging on my heart to alter my day. The dust will still be in the house tomorrow, and tomorrow is another day. As for the rest of the day, if I get busy I can still make it to the store and finish the piles of laundry. I pray you are able to bring your desires and your list of things to do in line with God's will for your life, at least for today. Take a walk with God and see some of the beauty He created just for you and He will meet you along the path.

LIGHTNING BUGS

Hot humid days are definitely not my favorite time of year, but when I complained as a child Dad always said, "Hot humid days make for a good corn crop." So, as a farm wife, I appreciate the hot humid days. During those humid days there is one small scene I look forward to each summer. It is the lightning bugs flashing their lights and hovering above the crops. There are usually a couple of nights where they are just gorgeous, and then they slowly dwindle away over the next few weeks.

There were hundreds of lightning bugs hovering over the corn field around our home last week. They remind me of new Christians. They are jumping around waving their arms saying, "Pick me! Pick me! I will help." I love new Christians in the church. They are so excited about their new faith, and want to be involved. Unfortunately, over time the excitement sometimes fades and occasionally Christian work becomes one more thing on their list of things to do. Why is that? If we are excited about Christ dying for our sins, we should remain excited until He calls us home. Serving with that excitement helps build the church and spread the Good News.

Sometimes we are so involved that we forget what is truly important. The most important thing is to become more grounded in God's Word. There are many precious scriptures to help us daily. Like those that give us peace in times of turmoil, and strength when we are weary. The truth is that sometimes Christian work can cause turmoil, and we always need God's strength to persevere. By all means, be involved and serve, but don't forget what is most important and that is growing in Christ.

I am reminded of the story of Martha and Mary in *Luke 10:38–42*. I am definitely a Martha, and for years I was offended that Jesus didn't send Mary to help her! I am sure some of you can relate. But I have come to love the story. I realize that God put this story in the Bible for people just like me. I am driven by details, organization and planning. But all the planning in the world doesn't matter, unless I seek God's wisdom and truth first. Jesus tells Martha this in verses *41–42, "My dear Martha, you are worried and upset over all these details! There is only one thing worth being concerned about. Mary has discovered it, and it will not be taken away from her."*

God gave me the skills to organize and plan for a reason. But He also gave me the gifts of faith, encouraging and shepherding so I would remember what is important. At times it is a constant struggle for me to step aside from the organizing and planning, and allow my service to glorify Christ. In lieu of that, I need to become less like Martha and more like Mary and seek God's will. I believe Martha struggled in this area as well, but Jesus never gave up on her. In *John 11:1–44* we read of the story of Lazarus being raised from the dead. Jesus asks Martha if she believes. Her response in *John 11:27* is, *"'Yes, Lord' she told him. 'I have always believed you are the Messiah, the Son of God, the one who has come into the world from God.'"* What a change! In Luke, Martha had a "me" attitude, but in John her focus is on Christ. I feel like she had a lightning bug moment. She lit up and said, "I get it! Pick me! I want to sit at your feet and learn and then I will go serve wherever you call."

If you are a Martha in a Mary world, maybe it is time you do what is most important. Sit back and watch the lightning bugs and say to God, "Pick me! I want to sit at your feet and learn today."

Don't let your light slowly dim, dig into God's Word and talk to Jesus. Yes, good works are important to help the church grow, but only when they are completed with a Mary heart.

<u>Suggested Scripture Reading</u>

- *Luke 11:38–42*
- *John 11:1–44*

 KNIT TOGETHER

God has such a wonderful way with words when He tells us in *Psalm 139:13* that He knit us together in our mother's womb. What does it mean to be knit together? Have you ever tried to knit? To me it is very complicated, yet my sister makes it look so easy. She clicks away with those needles and creates wonderful knitted items. I on the other hand, could never get the hang of it, and my projects were nearly unrecognizable. Knitting is not a talent I possess, nor do I have the desire to learn. But when God knits us together, we are complex and wonderfully made! *(Psalm 139:14)*. Each one of us is unique and beautiful in God's eyes.

Colossians 2:2 is another verse in the Bible where God talks about us being knit together with other Christians. I love this verse because it describes our relationship with other Christians as ties of love. But how does this compare to us being knit together by God? Let's do a little science research and learn more about human DNA. It is:

- Double Stranded
- The two strands are complementary
- The two strands are anti-parallel[c]

Our DNA is very complex. If you do an internet search on human DNA you will find many diagrams. These diagrams show how the two strands twist and wind, yet stay connected. Similar to an afghan my sister would knit. These two strands are complementary, or harmonizing. Yet they are anti-parallel which means they are going in opposite directions, like a receiving line. God created us using this very complex method, and wants us as Christians to be knit together in the same manner. It sounds just like the body of Christ! We are many people or strands. Each one of us has been given different talents and gifts, all headed in different directions in life. Yet we have one common bond, and that is Christ Jesus.

When a person becomes disconnected from the body of Christ, it creates a hole. It's very similar to a loose strand on a knit sweater. The sweater slowly starts to unravel, and before you know it, there is a hole. God does not desire holes in the body of Christ. He desires us to stay connected, each using our God given gifts and talents to mend the holes with ties of love.

Is there someone in your circle of friends, who has slowly become unraveled? Maybe it is time to mend the hole and knit them back into the circle with ties of love.

I want them to be encouraged and knit together by strong ties of love. I want them to have complete confidence that they understand God's mysterious plan, which is Christ himself.
Colossians 2:2

You made all the delicate, inner parts of my body and knit me together in my mother's womb. Thank you for making me so wonderfully complex! Your workmanship is marvelous—how well I know it.
Psalm 139:13–14

DEER AND FAWN

The other day when I stopped at a stop sign, I could see a deer walking along the edge of the field. I paused for a moment to see if she would come closer so I could get a better look. Then I noticed two small ears were sticking up above the soybeans directly behind the doe. Every time the mother deer took a step forward, the two little ears would take a step forward, tagging very closely behind. I didn't linger long, since she was protecting her fawn. It was also very obvious that she had no plans of turning in my direction.

As I described the scene to my husband I thought, "This is exactly what God desires from us!" He would love for us to follow so closely in His footsteps that every time He takes a step, we take a step. He is also there to protect us from danger, just as the doe is protecting her fawn. Jesus tells his disciples a parable about following in His footsteps.

> *"But the one who enters through the gate is the shepherd of the sheep. The gatekeeper opens the gate for him, and the sheep recognize his voice and come to him. He calls his own sheep by name and leads them out. After he has gathered his own flock, he walks ahead of them, and they follow him because they know his voice."*
> *(John 10:2–4)*

Just as the fawn was following her mother, Jesus expects us to follow Him. We are to know His voice and follow His lead. We need to look for opportunities to see where God is working and then we need to follow in His footsteps.

Psalm 18:33 says, *"He makes me as surefooted as a deer, enabling me to stand on mountain heights."* Christ enables us to do things which we can never do on our own. Not all Christian service is easy, but we are called to serve in ways which Christ makes possible. We need to remember that He is our strength and our reward is in heaven. Peter questions Jesus of this very fact in *Matthew 19*. Peter basically says, "I've given you everything I have. What's in it for me Jesus?" And Jesus replies, "Those who give up homes, family, and friends for my sake will receive much more. They will receive eternal life."

In our daily Christian walk, we need to follow in God's footsteps closely. No matter how easy or difficult the task, God promises protection just as the doe protects the fawn. He also provides strength like the deer when we set out to accomplish the more difficult tasks.

> *Then Peter said to him, "We've given up everything to follow you. What will we get?" Jesus replied, "I assure you that when the world is made new and the Son of Man sits upon his glorious throne, you who have been my followers will also sit on twelve thrones, judging the twelve tribes of Israel. And everyone who has given up houses or brothers or sisters or father or mother or children or property, for my sake, will receive a hundred times as much in return and will inherit eternal life. But many who are the greatest now will be least important then, and those who seem least important now will be the greatest then."* (Matthew 19:27–30)

Points to Ponder

- Where are you in your Christian walk?
- Can you see Christ's footsteps ahead of you?
- Are you taking a step forward every time Christ takes a step?

God's Change

Change has always been difficult for me. I'm just a comfort zone person. But I have learned over the years that change brought about by God is for the good. No matter how difficult the process. My decision to leave my career of twenty years to work part-time at our church was one of the most difficult decisions I ever made. Though I knew God was calling me to leave, I felt I was leaving a huge part of my life and my ministry behind.

Looking back I see that it wasn't my ministry to others I was afraid to leave, but the ministry others were giving to me which I was afraid to lose. I often reflect on the different people and the friendships I developed over the years. From one I learned leadership, and from another the true value of faith. I was given lessons in unconditional love, and how to be a prayer warrior. I learned the value of speaking kind words of encouragement, perseverance, and personal sacrifice. One great lesson was the importance of friendship. A friendship where you can just spill your guts about work frustrations one day, and then laugh together as you do a "happy dance" to celebrate an achievement the next. I feel so blessed to have worked with so many wonderful people, whom I also called friends.

As I was making my decision to leave, my prayers would change daily. One day I would pray for God to open doors so I could leave the stressful job. The next day, my prayer would be for God to remove the stress so I could stay with my friends. All the while, God was refining me as it says in *Zechariah 13:9, "I will bring that group through the fire and make them pure. I will refine them like silver and purify them like gold. They will call on my name, and I will answer them. I will say, 'These are my people,' and they will say, 'The LORD is our God.'"* God in His wisdom and omnipotent power moved me to a new and different place in my life. There have been times when the change has been difficult. I love my new job, but I miss my old friends. It took a quiet moment of reflection for me to realize that I did not leave the friendships behind. Of course I no longer see them daily, but they are a piece of my soul and a piece of my life. There isn't a day that passes, where I don't use a lesson I learned from those who crossed my path.

As Christians we need to take time to reflect on the wonders of daily life. God leads us through difficulties, happiness, unspeakable joy, friendships and much more. God uses other people in all these circumstances to help us, shape us and strengthen us. I am blessed for all God has done in my life. When I am feeling low, or confused, a short walk down memory lane reminds me that nothing in my life has been an accident. It was all part of God's plan. I know He is not finished with me yet, and there will be many more life lessons to learn. But for today, I love the fact that I can stop and count my blessings for the work He has done, the work He is doing, and the work He will continue to do in my life. Why? Because for me change is difficult, but when God brings about the change, it is always wonderful!

One day, I hope my friends will read this devotion and see the lesson or treasure they passed along to me. When they do, I hope they will be able to reflect on our friendship and what we learned from one another. God uses friendships to mold us and refine us. Those friendships even help bring about those difficult changes in life, as He prepares us for the next step in His grand plan.

BRIDGES OF LOVE

After watching the movie *The Bridges of Madison County*[d] starring Meryl Streep and Clint Eastwood, I found myself crying. Okay more like sobbing! I was somewhat embarrassed and thankful my husband had fallen asleep about thirty minutes into the movie. His disclaimer being there was a "lack of action" which one usually sees in Clint Eastwood movies. I wondered why this movie caused me to be so emotional. It definitely wasn't a Christian movie, since it is about a love affair between Francesca Johnson and Robert Kincaid. The movie had plenty of action from a woman's point of view, and I could feel the love between the two of them. As the movie ended, she decided to stay with her husband and her children. Even though I know it was the right decision for her to stay, my heart just broke as the love of her life drove away!

As I slowly quit crying and calmed my spirit, I began to pray. I asked God to reveal to me why the movie had touched me so deeply. At one point in the movie Robert describes his love to Francesca by saying, "This kind of certainty comes but once in a lifetime." I know in my heart, I have that certainty of love with my husband. Sometimes our busy schedules prevent us from expressing that love to one another, but I have the comfort of knowing with certainty that we love each other deeply.

I continued to pray as I felt God had more He wanted me to learn. Deep in my soul I felt God say to me, "Do you love me with this kind of certainty?" Ouch! Could I truly say I loved Christ as deeply as Francesca and Robert loved one another in the movie? Did I love God enough to go wherever He leads me with certainty? I wanted to say "Yes Lord, I love you," but I had to hesitate and search deep in my soul. I wondered to myself, do I?

I am reminded of the story in *John 21:15–17* where Jesus asks Peter three times *"Do you truly love me?"* Peter is quick to respond, *"Yes Lord, you know I love you."* But notice carefully how Jesus responds, *"Feed my lambs"* and *"Take care of my sheep."* If I truly love Christ, I need to love the church as I would love Christ *(Ephesians 4:15)*. I have to admit, some days that is very hard for me to do! My human nature has so many emotions. I not only have love, but hate and anger. I have trust but it is mixed with fear and apprehension.

God calls you and me to build bridges of love with certainty. It is a daily struggle to overcome my emotions and do His work. Every time my emotions show anger or fear, I need to be like Peter and say, *"Yes Lord, you know I love you."* But I also need to add, "Lord, help me to love others and build bridges of love for you, because I can't walk this road alone." Take time today to search your heart and your fears so you can build bridges of love in your life for Christ.

Suggested Scripture Reading

- *John 21:15–17*
- *Ephesians 4:15*
- *Romans 16:16a*
- *1 Corinthians 8:1b*

$\mathscr{S}$OCKS

Laundry. For the most part I don't mind doing laundry. Even when my boys were home, it didn't seem like a big chore, except for one load. The dreaded load of whites that included all those socks! Sometimes I just dread doing that load and wait until it is huge because I just don't want to sort through all the socks looking for the perfect match. But in reality, the bigger the load, the bigger the mess! Short socks, tall socks, inside out socks, his socks, her socks, pink stripes, blue toes, stained or worn out, brand new, holes (pitch that pair), you get the picture. You sort into piles, make matches and the last two socks aren't the same. Have you ever done that? Of course you have! That is why I keep an odd sock basket beside my dryer.

God blesses each of us with talents and gifts, but sorting through those gifts and finding your place in the body of Christ can be just as tedious as sorting a basketful of socks. Just because you have been given the gift of teaching, it doesn't mean that you can walk into a room full of middle school students (scary thought for me) and be an effective teacher. You have to develop your gift, nurture it, and refine it with the power of the Holy Spirit. Many Christians jump from one area of service to another without actually working to develop a plan. This reminds me of matching an inside out sock with what you believe to be the mate. It might be the right match, but you need to do a little extra work to be sure.

Sometimes we are given an odd combination of spiritual gifts, natural talents and personality traits. For those of us that fall into that category it can be very difficult to find a ministry that fits. For example, I am blessed with the gifts of faith, hospitality and administration. My natural talents and likes? They include a variety of items such as computer skills, writing, helping others, organizing. My personality is one that has compassion, a faithful friend, and eager to please. But I also have faith and strength to endure new things or solve problems. When I throw all this together, I sometimes feel like the odd sock basket. Where is my match?

If I strictly do ministry using my gift of administration, I am miserable. Though I am a very organized person, I need to be around people. My desire to help others, be with friends and help build their faith would go unused if I didn't incorporate them into my ministry. On the other hand, if I spent all my time helping others build their faith and being a hostess, I would be crazy because my life and household would be in shambles. Finding the right balance has taken a great deal of time, but I have learned that I also need variety. So what are some of the ways I have pulled these talents together for the glory of God?

I lead a ladies Bible study which brings me great joy. We learn together, laugh together and pray together. I have had many opportunities to share my faith and I love watching their faith grow as well. My husband and I host a small group. I have found that my house doesn't have to be spotless and decorated perfect to entertain guests. I let down my guard of perfectionism, and just enjoy fellowship with others. I also enjoy organizing large events. I am able to use my gifts of administration and hospitality to pull others together and form a team. My gift of faith helps create a focus or theme for the event. And when the event unfolds, my heart melts when lives are changed, which fuels my compassion for others.

God made each of us unique so that we could come together to be part of the body of Christ. So whether you are a new sock trying to find your way in ministry, or an inside out sock who is confused about your match, there is a place for you to serve. I recommend socks with pink stripes one day and blue toes the next. In other words, find a variety within ministry, so you won't become a worn out sock and suffer from ministry burnout. Maybe you are his and her socks and can serve together. If you are a holey sock and feel that you can't do ministry anymore, don't give up because God has a place for you.

Though sometimes we find it difficult to find our way, comfort can be found in *Psalm 139:1-18*. It is a beautiful reminder that our wonderful Creator made everything, including you, unique and with a purpose. May you read these words today and find comfort from an amazing God.

> *O LORD, you have examined my heart*
> *and know everything about me.*
> *You know when I sit down or stand up.*
> *You know my thoughts even when I'm far away.*
> *You see me when I travel*
> *and when I rest at home.*
> *You know everything I do.*
> *You know what I am going to say*
> *even before I say it, LORD.*
> *You go before me and follow me.*
> *You place your hand of blessing on my head.*
> *Such knowledge is too wonderful for me,*
> *too great for me to understand!*
>
> *I can never escape from your Spirit!*
> *I can never get away from your presence!*
> *If I go up to heaven, you are there;*
> *if I go down to the grave, you are there.*
> *If I ride the wings of the morning,*
> *if I dwell by the farthest oceans,*
> *even there your hand will guide me,*
> *and your strength will support me.*
> *I could ask the darkness to hide me*

and the light around me to become night—
but even in darkness I cannot hide from you.
To you the night shines as bright as day.
Darkness and light are the same to you.

You made all the delicate, inner parts of my body
and knit me together in my mother's womb.
Thank you for making me so wonderfully complex!
Your workmanship is marvelous—how well I know it.
You watched me as I was being formed in utter seclusion,
as I was woven together in the dark of the womb.
You saw me before I was born.
Every day of my life was recorded in your book.
Every moment was laid out
before a single day had passed.

How precious are your thoughts about me, O God.
They cannot be numbered!
I can't even count them;
they outnumber the grains of sand!
And when I wake up,
you are still with me!

$\mathcal{S}$HOWER CURTAIN

My sister Linda passed away this past year following a short battle with a rare blood disease. I have spent the last few months creating memories from some of her belongings. For some family members I created pillows from Linda's clothing and table linens. For other family and friends I made Christmas ornaments from her many handkerchiefs and doilies. Linda loved to quilt and sew. Though I am not the seamstress she was, I think she would have enjoyed my creations.

For myself, I made a shower curtain from her collection of silky scarves. When I look at the shower curtain, I see a square with flowers which reminds me of her love for her flower gardens. There is a block that looks like buildings. She loved to travel and maybe it reminded her of the many places she had been. One square looks like lines and rectangles, which is very fitting for her. She was a math teacher and geometry was her favorite subject. I can envision her falling in love with the scarf the moment she saw it. Another section is music notes. At one time Linda played the piano, and I remember her coming home from college and playing hymns for us.

There is one special block which reminds me of her the most. The design and bright colors resembles the '60s, an era when she was off to college. The rainbow in the middle is a symbol of Linda's hopeful spirit and faith. Linda always persevered. As the oldest of five, she desired to be the leader of the family. No matter how difficult the circumstances or challenge, Linda always reached for the pot of gold at the end of the rainbow. Not only in her daily life, but even during her final days before going home to see Jesus.

Sometimes I wish I could ask her more questions, such as her favorite Bible Story. I know she loved the writings of Paul and when she traveled to Greece, she said Paul's writings came to life. But when I think of Linda, I think of the story of Ruth and Naomi. Like many of us, Linda had some difficult times in her life, yet she persevered. Just like Naomi, she found peace with God. Peace that became a reflection of her sweet spirit. As a result, she shined bright with joy and kindness to others. There are also times when she reminds me of Ruth. Ruth worked hard to provide food for Naomi and herself. She was faithful to her mother-in-law and saw joy of serving God and others. Linda joyfully served in her church and showed kindness to everyone.

Linda's personality can be seen in many Bible characters, but her legacy is built on many Bible truths. Ironically, it is a legacy that is built on some of the common scriptures written by Paul. The first scripture which came to mind was the Fruits of the Spirit. Out of curiosity I thumbed through her Bible to see if she had possibly underlined that scripture. She had. I continued to look through her Bible to see what other verses may have impacted her life. Much of what she had underlined were in Paul's writings.

Below are a few of her favorite verses (*NIV*). None of them were a surprise to me. She was a teacher at heart, and lived life for others which is what these verses reflect. My prayer for you today is that you will apply these key verses to your own life. I pray that you will also live a legacy that others will desire to follow.

Love and faithfulness meet together; righteousness
and peace kiss each other.
Psalm 85:10

And hope does not put us to shame, because God's
love has been poured out into our hearts through
the Holy Spirit, who has been given to us.
Romans 5:5

But the fruit of the Spirit is love, joy, peace, forbearance,
kindness, goodness, faithfulness, gentleness and self-
control. Against such things there is no law.
Galatians 5:22–23

Serve wholeheartedly, as if you were serving the Lord, not people.
Ephesians 6:7

Preach the word; be prepared in season and out of season; correct,
rebuke and encourage—with great patience and careful instruction.
2 Timothy 4:2

ESTHER—GOD'S PRETTY WOMAN

One of my favorite movies is *Pretty Woman*ᶜ. There is just something inspiring about seeing Vivian played by Julia Roberts, transform from a prostitute into a beautiful, classy lady. There is a scene toward the end of the movie where Vivian is telling another prostitute Kit goodbye. Vivian has discovered a new strength inside herself and she plans to move to San Francisco in an attempt to make a better life. She invites Kit to join her, but her friend won't leave. Vivian encourages Kit to also make a better life and get off the streets.

Vivian says to Kit, "We think you have a lot of potential Kit De Luca." But Kit questions her saying, "You do? You think I got potential?" Vivian looks Kit in the eyes and says, "Oh yeah, don't let anyone tell you different!" Interestingly, in the next scene you see Kit telling her friend that she is looking into some beauty courses. She in turn encourages her friend to make a plan to get off the streets, because you can't live on the streets forever. Vivian sees potential in Kit, who in turn sees potential in someone else.

I'm reminded of the Bible story of Esther. Esther was raised by her Uncle Mordecai and she relied heavily on his guidance. Even though Esther was selected as a member of King Xerxes' harem and eventually became queen, she kept her Jewish identity hidden from the king. As the story unfolds, a law was put into affect where the Jewish people were to be slaughtered. Mordecai asked Esther to risk her life by going to the king to plead for the lives of the Jewish people. Esther of course was mortified, and felt very under qualified for the task at hand! I just love Mordecai's response to her in *Esther 4:13–14.*

> *"Don't think for a moment that because you're in the palace you will escape when all other Jews are killed. If you keep quiet at a time like this, deliverance and relief for the Jews will arise from some other place, but you and your relatives will die. Who knows if perhaps you were made queen for just such a time as this?"*

Esther certainly questioned her own abilities, but with a little encouragement from good old Mordecai she said, "Sign me up! I'll do it." She is definitely more eager than I am at times. I'm afraid to do the little events God tosses my way, and she was risking her life to save her people! Even though she committed to the task following Mordecai's encouragement, she still waited on the Lord's timing. She sends word back to Mordecai and the Jewish people to fast and pray for three days before she will approach the king. She patiently awaits God's timing to make her request known to King Xerxes and the Jewish people are saved.

What common lesson can we learn from these two very different stories? Encourage one another! Continually lift one another up in prayer, and follow God's lead. God knows we occasionally feel like we "lack potential," but God is a better encourager than Vivian, He sees the potential in all of us.

So what beauty classes are you signing up for this week? God has a plan for your life and knows your potential. Who knows if perhaps you were made queen for just such a time as this!

Mary Rodman

<u>Suggested Scripture Reading</u>

- *Book of Esther*
- *Proverbs 3:5–6*
- *Proverbs 16:9*
- *Psalm 5:1–3*

The Calf

I grew up on a dairy farm in central Ohio. Though life on the farm was busy, there were many lessons to be learned along the way. I'm sure I did my share of complaining about the work, but looking back over the years, I see how much the farm taught me about life and being a Christian.

One example which comes to mind is a premature calf. I remember the first time I looked at the little fellow. Never before had I seen a calf so small and fragile. He was so tiny Dad built him a pen out of straw bales. He was too little to be in the big pen with the rest of the calves and the bales gave him shelter and warmth. Part of my duties on the farm was to feed the calves and bed them with straw, but this little fellow was going to need extra special care. Dad was committed to helping him survive against all odds and between the two of us, we checked on him several times a day.

The love and care we showed the calf is an example of how much Jesus loves and cares for all of His children. There are many stories in the Bible which speak of Jesus caring for His sheep. In *Ezekiel 34:11–16*, we read how the Lord will find His sheep and rescue them. Dad rescued the calf from his mother, so we could provide a warm, safe environment for him to survive. In that same way, Christ longs to rescue us and meet our every need. So many people think they have to clean up their lives to come to Christ, when it is quite the opposite. Dad didn't wait to see if the calf could make it on his own. He brought him into the barn and cared for him.

Christ is longing to bring you into the barn and care for you. *John 10:14* says, *"I am the good shepherd; I know my own sheep, and they know me, just as my Father knows me and I know the Father. So I sacrifice my life for the sheep."* He was willing to die on the cross, just for you.

Christ loves and cares for His children. When we feel small, He will build us a safe pen from bales of straw. When we are hungry, He will provide nourishment for us. He is our Shepherd, just as Dad and I were shepherds to the small calf. Please allow Christ to care for you. Open your heart to His message of salvation, and allow Christ to lead you into the barn where it is safe and warm.

Suggested Scripture Reading

- Read *Ezekiel 34:11–16*
- Look up scriptures which refer to Christ as your Shepherd.

AILY FETCH

Our dog, Bailey, loves to play fetch. She will bring just about any toy back and play until she is literally exhausted. Her latest invention for fun is to drop her toy into the hot tub. Unfortunately for us it makes relaxing in the hot tub a little less enjoyable and oftentimes the toys come with grass and dirt attached. Bailey on the other hand, cannot wait for us to open the lid and let the fun begin. She is always eagerly waiting with a toy in her mouth ready to play when one of us heads that direction.

After Bailey puts her toy into the hot tub, she will pull herself up over the edge to watch. With her sad puppy dog eyes, she watches it swirl around in the hot tub hoping it will finally get close to someone. When it does, we will give it a toss across the deck for her to retrieve. One of her favorite toys is an empty pop bottle. When she drops one in, she will sometimes go to the next corner of the hot tub and retrieve it herself as it bobs along. As if she is saying, "I changed my mind. I want it back." And then she drops it in again.

There are days when she balances her pop bottle on the edge of the hot tub. Slowly she will nudge it with her nose, until it falls into the water. On some occasions she will select a toy that doesn't really swirl at all—it slowly sinks to the bottom as she stares in disbelief! That wasn't her plan at all because she desperately wants to play fetch. She will go to each corner and stare hoping to see her toy and get someone's attention to retrieve it for her. We of course do, and give it a toss and the fun continues.

As I was watching Bailey one day, it occurred to me that she is just like many of us. As Christians, there are occasions when we give our problems to God, or at least we think we do. We drop it in His cleansing water, but instead of walking away feeling relieved, we play fetch with God. We sit on the edge with our sad eyes and watch our problems swirl around. In reality, we are waiting for the right opportunity to retrieve the burden as it bobbles our way. Like Bailey, we want to chew on it and worry about it for a little while longer.

There are times when we bring our problems to God and they just sit on the edge. We have trouble deciding—do we want to keep them longer, or do we want to give them away?

What about the problems which sink to the bottom? Are you like Bailey? Do you sit on the edge in disbelief and wait for someone to give it a toss back to you? Or do you give it to God, let it sink into His open arms and walk away with a new sense of relief? *Psalm 68:19 (NIV)* says, *"Praise be to the Lord, to God our Savior, who daily bears our burdens."* **Daily**. What a key word in this verse! It doesn't say sometimes He bears our burdens, or when He's in the mood to play He bears our burdens. God doesn't sit in the hot tub and wait to see our reaction and give them a toss back when we desire. God's love is so great for us that His desire is to carry our burdens on a daily basis. For us, the hard part is to drop them in the pool and walk away. **Daily**.

I have a challenge for you today. Select a burden you are carrying and give it to God. If you would like, you can watch it bobble away and maybe even shed a tear or two if necessary. If you place it on the edge, that is okay. Just don't forget to give it a nudge before you walk away. Maybe the burden is so heavy it will sink to the bottom, in which case you can watch it slowly fade out of sight. Regardless, don't look over the edge and desire to retrieve it like Bailey desires to have her toy. Instead look to God, giving Him praise and thanks. Thank Him that He is willing to carry our burdens on a daily basis and promise Him that you will return tomorrow. When you return, don't retrieve your old problem, instead bring God a new "toy" to float, and watch another burden swirl away.

Bailey

HEDGE APPLES

Today I made my annual trip to the woods for hedge apples. The sticky, ugly, green, bumpy apple is supposed to keep spiders out of your house. Myth or truth? I can't really say, but I do believe it helps. I simply place them in the garage and basement on a piece of foil. They slowly dry and hopefully scare a few spiders away during the process.

Every year when I make my annual trip to the woods, it brings back a childhood memory. I chuckle to myself recalling the time Mom attempted to dry hedge apples for a craft. Mom enjoyed sewing, making crafts, arranging flowers and such. She read that you can take a hedge apple, cut it into round slices and dry the slices in a warm oven. Then you take the dried apple slices and make flowers. The picture of the dried flowers was quite attractive, so what did she have to lose? After all hedge apples grow wild and free, so she decided to give it a try.

As instructed, Mom placed the hedge apple slices in a warm oven to dry overnight. The next day, she turned on the oven to bake, forgetting about the hedge apples. Let me tell you that when hedge apples are baked in a hot oven, they smell horrible! To this day I can remember the nausea from the horrible odor. Mom opened the doors and windows. She turned on the fans, but she could not get that toxic smell out of the house for hours. Needless to say, that was Mom's one and only attempt at making hedge apple flowers.

While recalling my Mom's adventure, I had a very vivid picture (or should I say odor) of what it is like when you do ministry ahead of God, instead of waiting for His guidance. Sometimes it just plain stinks! Yes, I have done it more than once in my life. If you don't start with prayer and ask God for His guidance and blessings first, your beautiful vision can be a struggle to the very end. Maybe your vision is a local pantry, or feeding the homeless. Possibly it is an event at your church, or visiting a shut-in. Whether big or small, don't start without prayer. Ministry without prayer is difficult, but ministry following prayer has great results. Before you start, consider praying Nehemiah's words from *Nehemiah 1:5–6a "O Lord, God of heaven, the great and awesome God who keeps his covenant of unfailing love with those who love him and obey his commands, listen to my prayer! Look down and see me praying night and day for your people Israel."* Follow those words with your requests, petitions and ideas for ministry. This will open your heart to God's will for the ministry. Regardless of your dream or vision, your first step needs to be prayer. Then pray again, and pray some more. God will hear your requests, look down and lead the way because you asked Him to be a part of your efforts.

In my recent Bible study of Nehemiah, I learned that Nehemiah prayed for six months before he even approached King Artaxerxes for permission to return to Jerusalem to rebuild the city *(Nehemiah 1:1 and 2:2)*. Once in Jerusalem, he still did not reveal his plan to rebuild the wall around Jerusalem. His first priority was to access the situation and pray for guidance.

Gloria Gaither once said, "When we read of the great Biblical leaders, we see that it was not uncommon for God to ask them to wait, not just a day or two, but for years, until God was ready for them to act'." When it comes to ministry, oh how I would love to have the patience of Nehemiah, and other great Biblical leaders. We live in such a fast paced world. We want to move at lightning speed, even in our ministry. But God's ways are greater than our ways and waiting on His timing makes ministry smell like roses.

After the horrible smell, Mom never attempted to make hedge apple flowers again. However, I will continue to do God's ministry, by focusing on prayer as the first step. God will set a clear path for His work to be completed, when I pray first, listen, and then take action. Ministry will always take hard work and commitment, but oh the sweet aroma when lives are changed!

$\mathcal{F}$ALL COLORS

Sunday my husband and I had wonderful plans. We went to the early church service so we could take a drive and enjoy the beautiful fall colors. After arriving home, we packed a picnic lunch and promptly hit the road. We were about thirty miles from home when we realized there weren't many pretty colors to see. Occasionally we would see a glimpse of some gold, orange, or red in a forest, but for the most part we were seeing empty fields from harvest with bare tree branches in the distance. We were about a week too late. Since there was really no need to drive any farther, we ate our picnic lunch in a golf course parking lot with a window rolled down. It was chilly outside and we had lost our enthusiasm for our trip to view the fall colors.

Sometimes our Christian walks can feel much like our fall color trip—all gone, chilly, bare branches, empty fields, distant, and only glimpses of color. There are times in our lives when we feel like Christ is far, far away. We need to always remember Christ is never a week late. He is always right on time. When you study the story of Job you can feel his pain as he desperately searches for God. Yet Job never gives up hope and refuses to curse God.

There was a time in my life when I felt like Job. I had returned from a weekend spiritual retreat where I had poured myself spiritually, mentally, and physically into the life of a young lady. I desperately wanted her to understand just how much God loved her. It took more patience and strength than I had alone and I knew the Holy Spirit was with me the entire weekend. Following this weekend, for weeks and months God seemed so distant, with only glimpses of hope to brighten my world.

A pastor friend of mine encouraged me. She said to sing praises, continue to pray, continue to search and definitely do not give up hope. She understood and said that God was still there. He was stretching and growing my faith. I was unable to write devotions during that time. I felt as if my prayers landed on deaf ears, yet I kept knocking. I took her advice and played praise music, read God's Word, listened to great sermons on the radio, and attended church. Occasionally I would see a glimpse of God's beautiful colors, but those moments were so far and few between. It truly was a time of soul searching and growth, but like Job I never gave up.

It wasn't until I received a call to participate in another spiritual weekend retreat that I heard God's voice once again. When asked if I would help, I was scared and reluctant. What if God was still distant? How could I possibly show Christ's love through my actions and through the talk I was asked to present if I couldn't hear Him myself? Yet I could hear God's small voice whisper, "Just do it." I took a step of faith, and God was there! The silence I had felt for months seemed to disappear. As I prepared my talk for the weekend, God gave me His message for the ladies.

I don't know why God chose to stretch and grow me in this manner. Maybe it was to trim off some of the dead branches in my life. Or maybe so I would appreciate Him more during those chilly cold moments in life. All I do know is that Christ has never been more real. I have never felt His strength more since I stepped out in faith and said, "Ok, I'll do this one more time, but you better show up Lord because I can't do this on my own." God longs to hear the words, "Lord, I can't do this on my own." Paul conveys those exact words to us in *2 Corinthians 12:10, "That's why I take pleasure in my weaknesses, and in the insults, hardships, persecutions, and troubles that I suffer for Christ. For when I am weak, then I am strong."* Paul thanked God for his weaknesses because that is when Christ made him strong. I thank God for my months of stretching and searching, because that is when Christ taught me that I can't do it alone. My weakness is when Christ makes me strong.

Allow Christ to strengthen you today by taking the chorus of the old hymn, "I Surrender All^g"and turn it into a prayer. He will meet you and He will strengthen you in the days to come.

> "I surrender all,
> I surrender all.
> All to Thee, my blessed Savior,
> I surrender all."

MUDDY WATERS

You have read a previous devotion about our border collie, Bailey, and her love for floating toys in our hot tub so we will play fetch with her. Well there was one time when she was tempted just a little more than she should have been!

It was a warm day in late December, probably around fifty degrees, which is very unusual for us in Ohio. My husband and I decided to drain the hot tub and refill it to assure clean water the rest of the winter. My husband lifted the lid, hooked up the pump and started to drain it. Jim had to run an errand, so it wasn't long until he turned the job over to me. I was bustling around the house packing Christmas decorations back in their appropriate boxes and getting everything ready for storage. Suddenly I remembered the hot tub. I dashed outside to check the pump. You could not have prepared me for the sight I was about to see!

While I was bustling about the house, Bailey had been bustling about the yard and the barnyard. She was floating everything she could find in two feet of muddy, yucky water. It was so muddy the pump had even quit siphoning! I quickly said, "Bailey, NO!" She immediately stopped searching for toys to float, even though she didn't understand the problem. It was always okay to float her toys before, so why was this any different? I found pop bottles, a plastic plate, Frisbees, and the one that apparently had made the mess was a muddy, squished milk carton. Where in the world did she find that!

What started out as a simple game with Bailey, turned into a horrible problem which got her in big trouble that day. When I think about the muddy water she created, I realize how easily I can muddy the waters of my own life. The lack of a Bible study here, a missed prayer there, a little fib, some hurtful words, laziness—you get the picture. Before I realize it, my waters are as muddy as Bailey's mess she created in the hot tub. The good news is that when I ask for forgiveness, Christ will cleanse me.

There is a prophecy told in *Ezekiel 36:25–27* which speaks of Christ's forgiveness and the empowerment of the Holy Spirit when we come humbly to Him. These are powerful words which were spoken to the Israelites and prophesied about Christ and the promise of forgiveness!

> *Then I will sprinkle clean water on you, and you will be clean. Your filth will be washed away, and you will no longer worship idols. And I will give you a new heart, and I will put a new spirit in you. I will take out your stony, stubborn heart and give you a tender, responsive heart. And I will put my Spirit in you so that you will follow my decrees and be careful to obey my regulations.*

Overall Bailey is a very obedient dog and in her own way begs for forgiveness when corrected. She still has a pop bottle addiction, but we have set new boundaries so she is not tempted to go beyond the limit. If she brings us anything other than a pop bottle to the hot tub, we tell her, "No, go get a pop bottle." And she will search for the right toy. Christ will do the same in our lives. As we come to Him for forgiveness, He will help us set good healthy boundaries, so we will not be tempted to go beyond the limits. That is the power of the Holy Spirit within us. When we listen to the Holy Spirit, we will know which step to take in our lives so our waters will no longer be muddy.

I challenge you today. If your waters are a little muddy, come to Jesus and ask for forgiveness and He will cleanse you.

$\mathcal{B}$IRD POOP

This devotion is for my husband, Jim, because he said, "You can't write a devotion about bird poop." And when I told my friend Angie about my analogy she must have been speechless because she didn't even reply. But the next morning she had a good chuckle when she couldn't see out the rear window of her van because of all the bird poop.

Our deck continuously gets plastered with bird poop. At first we thought a gaggle of geese visited during the night. It was atrocious! Down the sidewalk, up the steps and all over the deck. Every day, I hose off the deck (multiple times), and they poop all over it again. The cycle just continues. We never see the culprits but there must be a lot of them based on the mess they are leaving behind!

Isn't life sometimes just like bird poop? You step into unexpected problems and what a mess. You feel like you are sitting in bird poop when shocking news comes your way. The worst is the unexpected bomb shells that take you by surprise. News like: Your spouse wants a divorce. Your teenager has a drinking problem. Your pregnancy ends unexpectedly. Your friend has cancer. Facing bankruptcy. Face it, sometimes life really is just like bird poop. We can wallow in it, or we can remember that there is One who will help lift us out of the mire and set our feet back on clean ground.

Take a look at the story of Abigail. Nabal was not your model husband and he definitely never won the husband of the year award! He was *crude and mean in all his dealings* (1 Samuel 25:3). She had to feel like she lived in bird poop, but she learned to make the best of a bad situation.

David and his men had protected Nabal's men while they were sheering sheep. In return David sent word that they were going to pass through the area. He requested that Nabal and his people please provide some provisions for them. But Nabal, in his selfishness, refused to share and as a result David planned an attack.

Now Abigail had just been pooped on one more time! Her and the people were about to be murdered because of her husband's bad attitude. Abigail didn't wallow in the poop. She didn't walk around worrying or pointing a finger at Nabal. Instead she stepped forward, developed a plan and sent the servants out to greet David and his men with a feast. As David approached, Abigail bowed low and begged him for forgiveness for her husband's lack of hospitality. David instantly saw the wisdom that she possessed. She was a hero for her quick thoughts and actions.

> *"Praise the LORD, the God of Israel, who has sent you to meet me today! Thank God for your good sense! Bless you for keeping me from murder and from carrying out vengeance with my own hands. For I swear by the LORD, the God of Israel, who has kept me from hurting you, that if you had not hurried out to meet me, not one of Nabal's men would still be alive tomorrow morning." Then David accepted her present and told her, "Return home in peace. I have heard what you said. We will not kill your husband."*
> *(1 Samuel 25:32–35)*

Abigail later told Nabal about the near disaster he had caused by his uncontrollable temper. The news caused him to have a stroke, and death shortly followed. Nabal was not the model husband, but to be a widow in biblical days was just another douse of bird poop. Abigail probably just wanted to say, "It is enough Lord!" The story doesn't tell us how she reacted but considering her past example, I'm sure she handled it with dignity and confidence. We do know that God rewarded Abigail for her heart of gold and her wisdom. When David heard of Nabal's death, he requested her hand in marriage and she quickly accepted.

Abigail was able to see beyond herself to the greater good of the people. She didn't focus on the bird poop that was dropping all around her. She focused on the big picture and the One who could rescue her from uncertainty. She wasn't a prestigious woman, but she was very wise and capable.

For your focus today, look past the bird poop of life and focus on the good that lies ahead. God will take all your poopy situations in life and turn them into good some day. He knows your past, your life today, and He holds your future.

Suggested Scripture Reading

- *1 Samuel 25*

ENS AND CHICKENS

There are hens and chickens that cluck and lay eggs, and there are hens and chickens which are plants. You often see these plants growing in unlikely places, like a pair of old work boots or a flowerpot with holes in it. They are a little bit like a cactus and pretty hearty, but they do like the sun. Several years ago a friend gave me about a dozen hen and chicken plants. I wanted to plant them under the bay window, but was told that it was unlikely they would grow there, due to the lack of sun. I decided that if they could grow in old boots and in holes, they should grow under the bay window. So I planted them there anyway. Within a couple of years they had multiplied like crazy.

This year we removed our paver sidewalk and put in a poured cement sidewalk and patio. The cement was also going under the bay window, so all the hens and chicks had to be replanted. I planted them in boots, flower beds, an old bird feeder, and an antique wash tub. I gave them to friends and family. My mom received a basket full for Mother's Day and I still had hens and chicks left! When the crew came to prepare for the cement, they asked about the plants. I told them I did not care about the remaining plants, and to throw them away. What did they do? They dug them up and put them in the grass for me. So, I planted hens and chicks in more unlikely places.

Just like the hens and chickens, God often calls unlikely people to be His disciples. He plants us in unlikely places, where we grow through unlikely circumstances. The women who followed Jesus were some of those unlikely people.

> *Soon afterward Jesus began a tour of the nearby towns and villages, preaching and announcing the Good News about the Kingdom of God. He took his twelve disciples with him, along with some women who had been cured of evil spirits and diseases. Among them were Mary Magdalene, from whom he had cast out seven demons; Joanna, the wife of Chuza, Herod's business manager; Susanna; and many others who were contributing from their own resources to support Jesus and his disciples. (Luke 8:1–3)*

The Jewish culture did not allow women to follow and learn from rabbis, yet Jesus took these unlikely woman along from village to village. Jesus didn't just allow these women to come along simply for financial support and to cook their meals. He had a greater plan! It was some of these same unlikely women who were the first to arrive at the empty tomb. What an unlikely circumstance for the women to be the first to hear the Good News that Christ had risen from the dead!

> *But very early on Sunday morning the women went to the tomb, taking the spices they had prepared. They found that the stone had been rolled away from the entrance. So they went in, but they didn't find the body of the Lord Jesus. As they stood there puzzled, two men suddenly appeared to them, clothed in dazzling robes. The women were terrified and bowed with their faces to the ground. Then the men asked, "Why are you looking among the dead for someone who is alive? He isn't here! He is risen from the dead! Remember what he told you back in Galilee, that the Son of Man*

> *must be betrayed into the hands of sinful men and be*
> *crucified, and that he would rise again on the third*
> *day." Then they remembered that he had said this.*
> *(Luke 24:1–8)*

These ladies not only financially supported Jesus' ministry, but they owed a great debt to Him because He had driven out demons and healed them. Their past circumstances brought them to an unlikely place during those days, the feet of Jesus. Women were not allowed in that inner circle with the rabbi, yet Jesus changed all of that. Not only were they in an unlikely place, but these faithful servants were blessed to be the first ones to spread the Good News about Christ's resurrection!

> *So they rushed back from the tomb to tell his eleven*
> *disciples—and everyone else—what had happened.*
> *It was Mary Magdalene, Joanna, Mary the mother of*
> *James, and several other women who told the apostles*
> *what had happened. (Luke 24:9-10)*

My hens and chickens were unlikely to grow where there was little sun, yet they flourished. We are all unlikely disciples, with unlikely circumstances, in unlikely places. But just like Mary Magdalene, Joanna, and the other women, time spent at Jesus' feet will turn our unlikely circumstances into a wonderful witness for what He has done. So stop waiting for the perfect situation to be a disciple and go spread the Good News!

$\mathcal{S}$TORMS OF LIFE

Last night we were awakened about 2:00 AM by one of those storms that absolutely lights up the sky and shakes the house. We recently moved into a new home with numerous sky lights, so there was no sleeping through the lightning, thunder, and wind. As I stepped into the living room, it was totally lit from the lightning in the sky. I paused just long enough to notice, and wonder just how safe I was from the lightning under the sky lights. My husband however, leaned back in his recliner, and watched the sky. Our cat Oreo was nowhere to be found, obviously she had already taken refuge under the furniture because it was too much for her to handle. But in spite of the intense storm, and our sleepy state, we thanked God for the much needed rain for our crops.

Reflecting on the evening, I see how the storm is just like the storms we face in our lives. When adversity comes your way, do you hide like Oreo, too afraid to face the unknown? Or maybe you are more like my husband. You face the storms with no fear at all, because you are so grounded in Christ you know He is by your side. No matter what life throws your way, you have to learn to step out in faith and face the thunderstorms, and hurricanes in life.

I face the storms in my life exactly how I faced the electrical storm. You will find me somewhere between the hider and the go getter. Cautious, careful, and reserved, yet trusting God is with me. However I'm a work in progress, because I used to be a hider. God continually teaches me through His Word to have more trust in handling the storms of life. I have also learned to thank Him in the midst of a storm, because He is building within me faith and strength for even greater challenges which lie ahead.

In the gospels we read about the disciples being fearful of losing their lives when their boat is being tossed around by a storm. They awaken Jesus afraid for their lives. Jesus calms the storm, and says to them in *Mark 4:40, "Why are you afraid? Do you still have no faith?"* There have been times in my life when God has spoken to me and said, "Where's your faith?" It is so much easier to look back on a situation, and see how God worked a miracle on my behalf, than it is to look forward with hope. But I'm learning to thank God in the midst of my storms, and ask Him to calm the seas, instead of waiting for the outcome to be thankful. After all, if He can merely speak, and calm a fierce storm raging in the skies, just imagine how He can calm the storms in my life, if I simply ask.

Points to Ponder

- Read one of the following: *Matthew 8:23–27, Mark 4:35–41, Luke 8:22–25.*
- What storms are you facing in your life right now? Have you talked to Jesus about them?
- Thank Jesus for the storms in your life, as they help you build a closer relationship with Him.

RANSFORMATION

When you read the following statements, how do you react?

- I just hate seeing Tommy get on the bus for Kindergarten. I just wish he could stay little forever.
- Oh, that new preacher removed the pulpit and speaks with just a microphone! He had a ladder up there one Sunday climbing up and down acting like a fool.
- I had to pack my office to move two doors down, just because of the new office layout.

Change in your life and change in your church. Do you welcome it or do you resist it? It can be very difficult whether you are moving two doors down, you miss the pulpit, or your baby is off to school. God is constantly transforming us, which in turn transforms the church. But no matter how difficult, godly transformation is good.

Richie McDonald was the lead singer for the famous country group, Lonestar from 1992 until 2007. Richie shared his testimony at an *Extraordinary Women* conference, where he was performing. God put it upon Richie's heart that the fame he was experiencing was not as important as his family. So he decided to step away from the fancy shows, the fame, the glory, and the busy schedule so he could spend more time at home being a husband and a father. I'm sure this was a difficult decision for Richie and his wife. I have no doubt the transition was difficult as well. Yet Richie says he has never regretted his decision to work less and be with his family more. God transformed Richie into a new person.

Godly transformation is good because we are allowing God to change us. Through the power of the Holy Spirit, you change your life style, grow in Christ, and get rid of bad habits. Change happens when you search the scriptures, pray and meditate on God's Word and allow Him to chisel away at you. The conversion makes you a better person, a person who can spread his or her wings and fly.

As people are being transformed, the church will be transformed as well. Once again, change is good and I love being part of a church which is doing exactly that. A church that is growing is full of Christians who are growing. Is it painful? Absolutely. Is change difficult? Absolutely. But God chisels at the church just like He chisels at our own hearts. Sometimes those traditions of speaking from the pulpit will not reach out to a new attendee like a visual example of a ladder. We have to allow God to shape the church just as we allow Him to shape us. We need to pray for Christ to mold and make changes in the church, so it will continue to grow and be appropriate for today's society. We don't step away from the truth which the Bible holds, but we need to let go of some traditions, for the sake of growth.

When my sons went off to kindergarten it could have been a difficult time for me. But I didn't allow this to happen, instead I celebrated life. I was excited for them. Excited to see them learn, make new friends and take their first bus ride. God was already chiseling at their lives and molding them into the adults which they have become. I wouldn't have missed these moments for the world.

Change in our lives, change in the office and change in the church are all difficult, but God is the Transformer of all. As we grow together, let us pray together, work together, love together and transform together.

> *But those who hope in the LORD*
> *will renew their strength.*
> *They will soar on wings like eagles;*
> *they will run and not grow weary,*
> *they will walk and not be faint.*
> *Isaiah 40:31 (NIV)*

Suggested Scripture Reading

- *Romans 12:2*
- *2 Corinthians 3:17–18*
- *2 Corinthians 5:17*

 TAR GAZING

My husband and I love to sit outside at night or in the wee hours of the morning and star gaze. God has blessed us with such a beautiful sight as we look up toward heaven. Neither of us are astrologers so other than locating the Big Dipper, to us they are just stars. Some seem very distant, others so close they glisten, and on a clear night they even appear to twinkle. Usually there are one or two stars which appear more prominent than others. I suppose they are actually planets, but for our enjoyment they are still stars. My husband seems to be the lucky one who will catch that quick glimpse of an occasional shooting star.

I wonder what the shepherds saw in the skies prior to the appearance of the Star of Bethlehem. They would not have had lights in the horizon from nearby cities as we do today. I can only imagine how many more stars they were able to see on a clear dark night. The sight must have been breathtaking. *Genesis 1:16–18* tells us that God not only made the sun and moon, but He also made the stars. He set them all in the skies to provide light for us. Maybe the shepherds actually used the stars for a sense of direction at night or to help them watch over their flocks.

Yet when the Star of Bethlehem appeared it was different. It was brighter and more prominent than any other star. *Luke 2:9* says an angel of the Lord appeared to the shepherds and a bright light shone around them. Could that have been the Star of Bethlehem? In *Matthew 2:7* Herod asks the wise men when the star first appeared.

It was bright enough to be seen hundreds of miles away. Where did it come from? Many years later, all we can do is wonder. We do know that God, who made the stars and the moon, had the ability to create one more star and place it in the sky to announce the birth of Jesus, if He so desired.

Regardless of our questions about the star and its miraculous appearance, we do know that the prophecies of Old Testament were fulfilled the day Christ was born and the star appeared. The news was announced to the shepherds first, and quickly traveled to Herod and the kings afar. The star was obviously an event which brought a lot of attention to the skies, and word spread that it was announcing the Messiah's birth. I love the fact that God didn't select the prominent Jews to be the first to hear of the Good News. He sent the angel to the shepherds. What a blessing to be the chosen ones. In selecting the humble shepherds, God was announcing to the world that all of us are worthy of the gift of salvation through Jesus Christ. What refreshing news for you and me, to know we are worthy of His love and compassion.

Maybe one day when we get to heaven we will know exactly what the Star of Bethlehem looked like, or maybe we will no longer care. For now I'm satisfied knowing that *Revelation 22:16* says, *"I, Jesus, have sent my angel to give you this message for the churches. I am both the source of David and the heir to his throne. I am the bright morning star."* The fact that Christ walked this earth, died for our sins, and will one day return, and reign as the Bright Morning Star is sufficient for me to put my faith in Him.

When you have the opportunity, gaze up at the stars and watch them twinkle. Let them serve as a reminder that Christ was born in Bethlehem, and died on a cross for the forgiveness of our sins. Raise your hands toward heaven and praise God for the Bright Morning Star. And if you happen to catch a quick glimpse of a shooting star, let it remind you that you too are worthy of Christ's love.

WELL DONE

We have the best dog in the world. We really do. Now on occasion she decides to remove boxes and other items from the garage and makes a mess in the yard. But as far as being a faithful dog, she is the best! Several years ago we moved a few miles down the road. We were concerned that Bailey would travel back up the road to the farm and not stay home. She knew her boundaries there and never left home. Upon her arrival, I walked her around the perimeter of our property and told her she was a good dog. The first night, we shut her in the shop so we wouldn't worry. Then the second night we let her sleep outside as usual. As we expected, she was right outside the door in the morning. A simple walk around her boundary line, and a little daytime exploring made her feel right at home. To our knowledge she hasn't left the property since, except for the occasional dreaded trip to the vet.

This morning she walked with me to the barn to put out food for her and the cats, which is our typical routine. I then decided to go for a walk, so I rounded the house and headed down the driveway. Without me saying a word, Bailey stopped at the tree which is her boundary line. Upon my return, there she was faithfully waiting. I called out to her, "Well done, you are such a good dog." She wagged her tail, grabbed her pop bottle to play, and off we went to the deck. To her it was worth the wait just to have a little play time.

Matthew 25:21 (NIV) says *"His master replied, 'Well done, good and faithful servant! You have been faithful with a few things; I will put*

you in charge of many things. Come and share your master's happiness!'"
Well done, my good and faithful servant. Can Jesus say this about
your life? Bailey knows her boundaries, but do we? We like to test
God, push rules to the limit, and twist the truth slightly to fit
our needs. God has blessed us with intelligence and the ability to
reason. Along with that He also gave us free will to make choices.
Fortunately when we make bad decisions, He gives us grace to cover
our mistakes. None of us are perfect, but we need to strive to do
better on a daily basis. Better at serving Christ, and better at helping
others.

God rewards us with praise, just as I do Bailey. I told her she
did a good job, and gave her a pat on the head. As a reward, we also
played fetch for a few minutes. These are all things she loves. God
loves to bless His children in the same manner. When we reach out
to someone in need, we are blessed with a filled heart from serving
others. When we pray for others, we are blessed by spending time
with God. Each day is different, and each day God puts witnessing
opportunities in front of us. In order to see these opportunities, we
simply need to slow down our lives, and live in the boundaries God
sets. In other words, sit by our tree waiting, and listening for the
Master. We need to practice the words of *Psalm 37:7a*, *"Be still in the
presence of the LORD, and wait patiently for him to act."*

So take a few moments before starting your day, and ask God
for the opportunity to minister to someone today. When your day
comes to an end, take time to pray. Thank him for the blessing of
serving Him and ask forgiveness for any opportunities you may have
missed along the way. As you listen to God, I am sure you will hear
Him say, "Well done, my good and faithful servant! Wait till you
see what I have planned for you tomorrow!"

LESSINGS

Blessings I do not deserve,
For time spent with those I serve.

Blessings lead to happy days,
As I worship God in praise.

Blessings flow from up above,
Land upon me like a dove.

Blessings from the One who reigns,
My Lord who helps me sustain.

Blessings fill me with great joy,
For my heart He does employ.

Blessings make my life complete,
Till my Lord one day I meet.

$\mathcal{S}$URVIVOR

Are you a survivor? Country music recording artist Reba McEntire recorded a song several years ago titled, "I'm a Survivor[h]." The words to the song have always touched me because I can relate to them. We all face difficulties in our lives, but as a result we grow into stronger human beings. Maybe you can relate to some of these lyrics: "The baby girl without a chance." "A single mom who works two jobs." "A victim of a circumstance."

I've always considered myself a survivor when difficulties come my way. But when I think about it, surviving has very little to do with me. It has everything to do with my God, my family, and my friends. I have some very dear friends who have made *Colossian 2:2* come to life for me recently. It says, *"I want them to be encouraged and knit together by strong ties of love. I want them to have complete confidence that they understand God's mysterious plan, which is Christ himself."* When I have difficult times or difficult decisions, I can count on these ladies to knit together with me and lift me in prayer. They remind me that God is in control of every detail of my life.

When I was struggling as a single mother years ago, my family was my lifeline of support. Had it not been for my parent's love and support, I would have been the single mom working two jobs to survive just like the song describes. I love the line in Reba's song, "But I must have had my Mama's will and God's amazing grace." But I find more survival skills in God's Word. Her song has become a reminder to me to search the scriptures during those times in my life and not to rely on my own understanding *(Proverbs 3:5–6)*.

There are so many verses which remind us that He is our source of strength and our Guide. Verses like, *Psalm 66:9, "Our lives are in his hands, and he keeps our feet from stumbling."* Or during those difficult times leaning on *Deuteronomy 4:37a (NIV) "He brought you out of Egypt by his Presence and his great strength."* There is such comfort knowing God will lead me through many difficulties during my lifetime.

As I look back over my life, I see where every trial has made me stronger, but more importantly it also made me weaker. Weaker, because I learned the best way for God to strengthen me is to let my weakness show, and give Him total control. By totally putting everything in God's hands, I have grown to realize that in my weakness, He is my strength *(2 Corinthians 12:9–10)*. Yes, I'm a survivor, but more importantly, I survive because He is my Guide, my Comforter, and my Strength.

Suggested Scripture Reading

- *Isaiah 33:2,*
- *Isaiah 40:29–31*
- *Psalm 23:3*
- *Acts 14:22*
- Find bible verses which talk of God's strength and guidance. Memorize them so you hold His truth in your heart during the difficult times in life.

MISSED ROADS

In our travels this year, there were two times we missed a turn. The first time, I was driving and Jim looked at the map to reroute us. Our new route was a beautiful, steep, winding mountainous drive. At one point we passed a huge, gorgeous canyon on our left. Jim was absolutely amazed at the view. He remarked of its beauty and was in awe. Unfortunately there was no place to pull off, and I was unable to see much due to the treacherous driving. Since he usually does the mountain driving, I was glad that he was able to enjoy the scenery for a change.

The second incident was beautiful but in a very different way. Jim missed the exit and it was my turn to get us back on course. I instructed him to take the next exit from the freeway, and to turn left onto 7 Mile Road. Now 7 Mile Road was a Montana dirt road and Jim promptly asked how far. I told him that my best guess was about seven miles, or a little more than a quarter of an inch on the map. It depends on how you want to look at it. The road led us past some crops, which he enjoyed. It seemed to ease his frustrations of being on a dirt road, as we bounced along and the dust was flying. The farther we went down the road, the more beautiful it became. We had mountains in the distance, but the real beauty was along the side of the road. Lining both sides were yellow wild flowers which resembled small sunflowers. They were in full bloom and they were everywhere.

In our lives we often miss a turn, but God takes all our missed turns and makes them into something beautiful. You may have a huge canyon off the side of your road. A canyon caused by a bitter divorce, abuse, or an addiction. When you look back, you realize that God made something beautiful out of your messed up life. The beauty of the canyons in our lives is that God wastes nothing. He will one day use your canyon to help others.

The wild flowers remind me of those little bumps in the road. You travel along your 7 Mile Road, the dust is flying, but you know there is an end in sight. You are always able to focus on God because He has sprinkled some cheer along the way. You may experience a fight with your children, but God allows you to turn that into a teaching moment. Maybe the loss of a loved one, but knowing they are in heaven somehow brightens your path as you mourn. God uses all the moments in our lives to direct our paths.

I am reminded of the story of Jesus and the Samaritan Woman *(John 4:1–42 NLT)*. She traveled a dirt road every day to draw water from the well. I don't think she was seeing bright flowers along her path, as she lived in shame. Jesus knew everything about the Samaritan Woman, yet he asked her for a drink of water. How shocking this must have been to this lady since Jews didn't even talk to Samaritans! By simply talking to her, Jesus instantly planted a wildflower along her path. When Jesus asked her to go get her husband, she said she had none *(vs. 17b–18 NLT)*. *"Jesus said, 'You're right! You don't have a husband—for you have had five husbands, and you aren't even married to the man you're living with now. You certainly spoke the truth!'"* In one sentence Jesus revealed her canyon! But He didn't stop there. He used the Samaritan Woman to be a witness to the entire town.

> *The woman left her water jar beside the well and ran back to the village, telling everyone, "Come and see a man who told me everything I ever did! Could he*

> *possibly be the Messiah?" So the people came streaming*
> *from the village to see him. (John 4:28–30)*

God turned her canyon into something beautiful. In the past she had lived in shame, now she went to tell everyone that she had found the Messiah. Many others in the village believed in Jesus because she was a witness to what Christ had done for her *(vs. 39–42)*. This is a lady who had lived in shame her entire life, yet Christ used her in a mighty way. Maybe it is time for you to allow God to change your canyon into something useful and beautiful. Maybe it is time for you to pick a few flowers along the way as you come to the end of your 7 Mile Road. Take time to hand someone a flower and tell them what Christ has done for you.

Suggested Scripture Reading

* *John 4:1–42*

MOTORCYCLES AND BISON

This year we vacationed in Yellowstone National Park. It is very common to see bison roaming the plains and walking along the roadsides. While we were traveling in a valley one evening there were nearly twenty-five bison blocking the road. Traffic was at a standstill in both directions. The herd was actually moving toward us, so the cars on our side of the road were slowly backing up. Jim and I had our windows open enjoying the moment. I was about to lean out the window for a good photo when all of a sudden the two motorcycles leading the oncoming traffic decided it was time to get moving. They were probably two of the bravest motorcyclists I have ever seen. They revved their engines and started beeping their horns. The next thing we knew, there was a stampede of bison in our direction! We immediately put up our windows, looked at each other and then chuckled. Like putting the windows up was going to save us from the stampede! The bison were so close that I could have petted a big ole boy as he ran past, if I had been brave enough to open my window again. Fortunately no one was hurt and in reflection, it was fun to watch. But I still wonder, "What made the motorcyclists so brave?"

We witnessed the exact opposite reaction the following morning. There was one big ole bison walking down the road toward a motorcycle in front of us. The driver promptly stopped and started pushing his motorcycle backward with his feet. The bison would take a few steps forward, and the motorcycle pushed his bike backward.

The bison would step forward, the motorcycle pushed backward. Again and again this happened as the bison continued to march toward the motorcyclist. Soon the driver of a minivan came to his rescue. It drove around us and wedged the van between the bison and the motorcycle. As a result, the bison turned off the road and into the valley. Obviously this motorcyclist was not as brave as last night's drivers!

We witnessed two very different reactions to bison, yet as Christians we are very similar in our ability to witness. Sometimes Christians can be too bold and too pushy in their faith. This can cause a "stampede" as non-Christians turn and run the other direction. Yet backing away from non-Christians like the second motorcyclist backed away from the bison, isn't the answer either. This can sometimes portray an, "I am better than you attitude." It can make non-Christians feel as if Christians don't care about their well being or want to associate with them. God wants us somewhere in the middle, building the relationships and leading the lost to Christ. We can't do this on our own. We need to rely on the Holy Spirit to lead us in acts of kindness and to speak the gospel to others. If you follow the letters of Paul, he shows his compassion for others throughout scripture.

> *When I arrived in Troas to proclaim the Message of the Messiah, I found the place wide open: God had opened the door; all I had to do was walk through it. But when I didn't find Titus waiting for me with news of your condition, I couldn't relax. Worried about you, I left and came on to Macedonia province looking for Titus and a reassuring word on you. And I got it, thank God! (2 Corinthians 2:12–14a MSG)*

What compassion he had for the Corinthians and for Titus! Continuing on in Paul's second letter to the Corinthians, he speaks about being used by God as a witness. He declares himself inadequate to preach the gospel. In fact, it is only through the power of the Holy Spirit that he is able to preach the gospel.

> *In the Messiah, in Christ, God leads us from place to place in one perpetual victory parade. Through us, he brings knowledge of Christ. Everywhere we go, people breathe in the exquisite fragrance. Because of Christ, we give off a sweet scent rising to God, which is recognized by those on the way of salvation—an aroma redolent with life...We stand in Christ's presence when we speak; God looks us in the face. We get what we say straight from God and say it as honestly as we can. (2 Corinthians 2:14b–17 MSG)*

God calls us to care for one another as Paul cared for Titus and the Corinthians. He also calls us to spread the Good News to the unsaved. I pray you find yourself somewhere in the middle. Not the person who causes a stampede, nor the one who backs away from witnessing in fear. May you seek God's guidance and strength and be filled with the Holy Spirit as you build relationships and witness of God's saving grace.

Bison in Yellowstone National Park

ᗞUST BUNNIES

It seems like no matter how hard I try to be a good housekeeper, I still have dust bunnies. Maybe I should call them dust kitties in our home. With two house cats, the balls of fur and dust seem to accumulate frequently. From time to time when I'm not in the mood to clean, I find myself blaming my son for the dust bunny problem. After all it was he who brought both kittens into our home, batted his blue eyes and said, "Can I keep it?" Well what is a mother to say, except a reluctant, "Yes."

Of course many years later, my son has moved out, and what did he leave behind? Two cats! In an honest attempt to find them a new home I periodically remind him that they are his cats. I have to admit I do enjoy their company, and I would miss them if they moved. I guess you could say the cats, and the dust bunnies they create have taken permanent residence in my home, and my heart.

Do you have dust bunnies? What about dust bunnies in your heart? I'm referring to feelings of an unforgiving heart. Many times there is pain from our past which has taken up permanent residence in our hearts. We can sweep the dust bunnies under the carpet of our heart for years. An unforgiving heart can eat at your spirit as it festers, but God commands us to forgive one another. When Peter asked Jesus how many times he should forgive his brother, Jesus replied *"seventy times seven" (Matthew 18:21–22).* This was Jesus way of saying not to keep a record of wrongs, and to always forgive with a repentant heart. When we confess our unforgiving heart to God, He will slowly heal us, and change our hearts.

We live in a "me" society today, which tells us to focus on our pain, and our feelings. But Christ calls us to focus on the pain, and feelings of others. There are times in my life when I have prayed for someone who has hurt me. Yes, at first the prayers are curt, short, and still full of blame. Eventually Christ softens my heart, and my prayers become more meaningful. As my heart starts to forgive, the blame shifts from the one who hurt me, to my own sin in the situation. When I take the "me" out of the equation, and think about them, I suddenly forgive.

There is a great passage of scripture in *Romans 12:9–21(NIV)* which tells us how to treat others. Among those verses are passages which say:

> *Be devoted to one another in brotherly love.*
> *Be…faithful in prayer.*
> *Bless those who persecute you.*
> *Live in harmony with one another.*

If we truly follow this scripture, we have to forgive just as Christ has forgiven us. So maybe it is time for you to get out your dust buster, and clean up the dust bunnies of your heart. It is okay if your prayer begins curt and full of blame, Christ will stand beside you, and lead you to forgiveness. Be patient, be persistent, and be prayerful because God will cleanse your heart and bind you together in harmony.

> *Since God chose you to be the holy people he loves, you must clothe yourselves with tenderhearted mercy, kindness, humility, gentleness, and patience. Make allowance for each other's faults, and forgive anyone who offends you. Remember, the Lord forgave you, so you must forgive others. Above all, clothe yourselves with love, which binds us all together in perfect harmony. (Colossians 3:12–14)*

URPLE BARN

Being married to a farmer can be a lesson in directions, and faith at the same time. There are often times when my husband will send me on an errand, or request my presence in a field which I have never entered before. I will receive directions like, "Go through the little town, around a curve or two there will be a purple barn. Go past the barn, turn north, and then take the third road to the east. Now if you pass two corn fields, you went too far."

Ok, so maybe I'm exaggerating a bit as I have never seen a purple barn, but it might help if we had such landmarks, because they would be much easier to find. Plus after numerous curves, and turns, which direction is north? I haven't a clue unless the sun happens to be rising or setting. I have learned over the years to take such directions with a grain of salt, don't stress, and head in the general direction. Most likely it will be through the town, and around more than a couple of curves. I find my destination, or thank the Lord for the invention of cell phones, so I can call my husband for more clear directions.

Have you ever felt like God's directions for your life are just as vague? I often find myself wondering if I'm doing God's will. It would be so much easier if God would just use a 2x4 board to get my attention! It is so easy to choose the activities in life which I enjoy, but it is a little more difficult to follow through with some of the plans God has for my life. I have always liked the protection, and safety of working within my own limitations. But just like I have grown as a farmer's wife, I have grown as a daughter of the King. I find Him constantly challenging my limitations, and stretching me.

Just as I used to worry about getting lost, I used to worry about failing God when He asked me to step out of my comfort zone. The good news is GRACE! God doesn't expect me to be perfect. He just wants me to try, and give the task my best effort. The more God challenges me to step out in faith, the greater my love is for Him. It is His way of stretching, and growing me throughout my Christian walk. I find I can't go through life without seeking His direction.

To build confidence, I continually remind myself of Bible verses like *Jeremiah 29:11* or *Proverbs 3:5–6.*

> *For I know the plans I have for you," says the* LORD. *"They are plans for good and not for disaster, to give you a future and a hope.*

> *Trust in the Lord with all your heart; do not depend on your own understanding. Seek his will in all you do, and he will show you which path to take.*

When I step out in faith and follow God's directions for my life, the road isn't quite so curved, and I can clearly see which direction is north. Take time each day to know God's plan for your life, and He will give you landmarks just like the purple barn.

Points to Ponder

- What direction is God leading you today?
- How will following Christ deepen your relationship with Him?

Suggested Scripture Reading

- *Hebrews 11*
- *Psalm 16:11*
- *Psalm 17:5–6*
- *Proverbs 2:7–10*

A DAY WITHOUT STANLEY

The weather has been a little rainy lately. Actually the weather has been extremely rainy for weeks, which puts a damper on farming. Regardless, there is always work to do in the shop, or equipment to prepare for the next job.

Yesterday when Jim came home from the barn, I began our normal conversation. "What did you and Stanley work on today?"

"I haven't seen or talked to Stan all day," Jim replied.

"Well that's unusual. A day without Stanley is almost like a day without Jesus. Isn't it?"

"Close, but not quite."

Stanley is our neighbor, who also farms. He and Jim share equipment and labor, and farm a few acres together. So unless we are on vacation, they work together or at least talk almost every day. They are making plans, discussing farming or fixing something.

A day without Stanley is unusual, and sort of like a day without sunshine. But a day without Jesus is a totally different story. If Jesus isn't a part of your daily routine, where do you turn when things get hectic or unorganized, or tempers flare and frustrations build? Unfortunately we often lash out at those we love the most. Often this causes problems at our jobs, or tension in our families. If we learn to change our focus to Jesus, many of our big problems become much more manageable because He gives us strength for each new day *(Philippians 4:13)*.

God created us in His image *(Genesis 1:27)* so that we would be His companions and worship Him. We can either worship God or worship others and our busy lives. When Satan was tempting Jesus in the desert he said, *"I will give you the glory of these kingdoms and authority over them... because they are mine to give to anyone I please."* but Christ quoted scripture and replied, *"You must worship the LORD your God and serve only him" (Luke 4:6–8).*

So what do you worship each morning? Do you stumble toward the kitchen for that first cup of coffee and sit aimlessly staring as you wait for the caffeine to kick in? Or maybe you rise quickly, shower, and grab coffee as you hustle off to work, just to sit in a frustrating traffic jam. When you rise each morning, what is on your mind? Social media? Today's schedule? World news? Jesus?

Maybe at noon you work through your lunch or pause briefly to visit with a co-worker. The work day has ended, but your day is far from over! Soccer Mom for your children. Workout at the gym. Mow the grass. Fix supper. Do the dishes. Walk the dog and feed the cat. Little Johnny and Susie need a bath. Check their homework. Goodnight stories. And finally last week's episode of your favorite TV show! A 2:00 AM feeding, and your day starts over again at 5:00 AM! No matter our stage of life, we all lead busy lives.

Do you ever lay your exhausted head down at night and wonder, "Where was Jesus today?" Well, Jesus was there when you had that first cup of coffee. He was in the traffic jam. He helped you shuttled the kids and give them a bath. Believe it or not He was beside you all day long! The question we truly need to ask ourselves is, "When did I miss an opportunity to see Jesus today or talk to Him?" We can either let our lives control us, or we can take control of our lives by making time for Jesus.

Christ longs for a relationship with you and He longs to be a part of your busy life. Invite Him into your busy schedule. He longs for a daily relationship with you. Take a few moments to focus on your own life and come up with some creative ways to spend more time with Jesus. Below are a few suggestions which might help you get started. Remember a day without Stanley is like a rainy day with no sunshine, but a day without Jesus can seem out of control!

<u>Time with Jesus Tips</u>

- Rise 15 minutes earlier to have a quiet time with Jesus.
- Keep a prayer list in your car and pray for others when stuck in traffic.
- Teach your children a Bible verse each week during the bed time story.
- Sing your favorite Christian song or hymn while you shower.
- Listen to the Bible or a Christian book while doing your workout or mowing the grass.
- Have a lunch date with Jesus one day a week.
- Take time to enjoy a hike in nature.
- Enjoy a sunrise or sunset.
- Thank Him for your wonderful life and the blessings you have been given each night.
- Sing "Jesus Loves The Little Children" and "Jesus Loves Me" during the 2:00 AM feeding.

ALF

When I first met my husband, he owned a dog named Alf. I'm not sure why Alf was named after the old TV sitcom. He was a pretty good farm dog, but he had one slight problem. He didn't like to stay home. Maybe he really was an alien, and he was looking for the planet of Melmac where the original Alf was from. If he was off of his chain, he was on the run. One of the places Alf liked to go was across the field to the creek.

On one occasion when Alf was missing, Jim went to the creek looking for him. In hopes that he would return, Jim yelled, "Alf! Come here Alf! Alf! Come here Alf!" He yelled over and over, without any success. Well if you cross the creek, there is another field, and then a couple of neighbors live on the next road. What they heard on their side of the creek was, "Help! Come here help! Help! Come here help!" Like any good neighbor in the country, one of them jumped in a truck, and quickly drove around the block. He flew down the lane to the creek expecting to find Jim injured or hurt. He came running to Jim and asked him what was wrong and should he call for help. Jim was a little shocked and replied something like, "Hurt? I'm not hurt. I'm looking for my dog. Alf ran off again." As the neighbor's adrenalin quit pumping, they enjoyed a good chuckle together. Jim recalls this story frequently, and remembers the impact it had on him that neighbors tried to come to his rescue the day he called for Alf.

As Christians, how many times do we take advantage of our Good Neighbor, Jesus Christ? He is there for us, if we simply call out to him. "Help! Come here help!" Sometimes it is easier to wallow in our own problems, pain, or misery than to talk to Jesus. Instead of being miserable, and worrying, we need to pour our hearts out to God in prayer.

One biblical example of a person who poured her heart out to God in the midst of her misery is Hannah. We can read about her heartache in *1 Samuel 1*. Elkanah had two wives, Peninnah who had children and Hannah who did not. As a family, they would make yearly trips to the temple to sacrifice and worship. Peninnah was very cruel to Hannah and reminded her constantly that God had not given her any children. On one trip to the temple, Hannah poured her heart out to God. We read of Hannah's misery in *1 Samuel 1:10–11*.

> *Hannah was in deep anguish, crying bitterly as she prayed to the* LORD. *And she made this vow: "O* LORD *of Heaven's Armies, if you will look upon my sorrow and answer my prayer and give me a son, then I will give him back to you. He will be yours for his entire lifetime, and as a sign that he has been dedicated to the* LORD, *his hair will never be cut."*

Hannah was truly crying out to God. I love how The Message describes Hannah's mental state. *"Crushed in soul, Hannah prayed to* GOD *and cried and cried—inconsolably."* Have you ever been so troubled in your soul that you felt as if you were being crushed? She was pouring out her heart and soul to the only One who could provide her comfort.

God heard Hannah's prayers and granted her a son, whom she named Samuel. Once Samuel was old enough, she dedicated him to the Lord as she promised, and left him at the temple. The God who heard Hannah's pain, and sorrow is the same God who will hear you. You don't have to wait until your soul is crushed, call out to the Good Neighbor today. He will hear your cry, "Help! Come here help!" Open your heart to the One and only true Healer for your soul.

HEART OF WORSHIP

Honor the Lord for the glory of his name. Worship
the Lord in the splendor of his holiness."
Psalm 29:2

O God, we meditate on your unfailing love
as we worship in your Temple.
Psalm 48:9

Everything on earth will worship you; they will sing
your praises, shouting your name in glorious songs.
Psalm 66:4

Happy are those who hear the joyful call to worship, for
they will walk in the light of your presence, Lord.
Psalm 89:15

Come, let us worship and bow down. Let us
kneel before the Lord our maker.
Psalm 95:6

Worship the Lord with gladness. Come before him, singing with joy.
Psalm 100:2

Several years ago Michael W. Smith released a song, "The Heart of Worship[i]." It talks of worship being more than singing a song. So many times we consider worship to be the praise and worship time on Sunday mornings as we sing our favorite hymn or praise song, but it is so much more. According to the internet the word worship is defined as the following: "The reverent love and devotion accorded a deity. The ceremonies, prayers, or other religious forms by which this love is expressed. Ardent devotion; adoration[i]." Nowhere in this definition does it say, "Singing your favorite songs."

Many times we think of worship as what makes us happy. The true definition is expressing our love, and devotion to God. It shouldn't matter what song we sing on Sunday, or what the message is about. If I get upset because we didn't sing my favorite hymn, or the message was inappropriate for me, then I truly don't have a heart of worship. It's not about me, it is about Him!

A true heart of worship isn't only on Sunday mornings either. It should be a part of our daily lives. Some days I find it hard to empty myself, be still, and truly focus on all God has done for me. But when I sneak away to have a quiet time with God, I truly treasure those moments! It might be on Sunday morning as I tune out the world, a quiet moment at home, or a slow walk. But when the focus is on God, and I have a heart for worship it is so refreshing. There is something amazing about focusing on Christ. It changes my view on life.

As the song lyrics say, I challenge you today to "Come back to the heart of worship." Express your reverent love to God and He will show you all the wonderful ways in which He cares for you. Take a few quiet moments to reread the scripture references above. Truly focus on God with a heart of worship, and remember:

*Happy are those who hear the joyful call to worship, for
they will walk in the light of your presence, Lord.*
Psalm 89:15

$\mathscr{S}$TEPDADS

Being a stepfather is such an important yet difficult role for a man. I speak from experience since my husband, Jim, has been a stepdad for over twenty-five years. And might I add that he is a great one! Their role is sometimes to act as the father by nurturing, loving, and disciplining. Yet there are other times when the biological father steps into that role, and they are expected to take a back seat to parenting. This has to be very difficult, yet God has called many men and women into family leadership under these circumstances. I look from the sidelines and realize how much sacrificial love it takes to be a Christian stepparent to children! Many children desperately need this influence in their lives, and many men and women have taken on this challenge in today's society.

I have friends who are raising a split family. This gentleman has stepped up to the plate as a wonderful Christian stepdad. He is truly a father to them in every sense of the word. The young girl's biological father disappeared from her life for about six weeks, and she was hurt and angry. When he suddenly reappeared, she decided to go see her father. Understandably, her stepfather was crushed! I can only imagine his pain. I am sure thoughts were running through his head like: I am always here for you. I support you financially. I love you unconditionally. I would never walk away, for any period of time. Why do you want to see him again? You know he doesn't love you like I do.

How do I know this? I have seen this same pain in my own husband's eyes from time to time.

As a young girl, she is torn between the two fathers in her life. She longs for a relationship with her biological father. Yet she loves her stepfather, who she sees daily. But as a stepfather, he has to let go of his own pain, and allow her to leave, praying she will not be hurt once again. This is truly sacrificial love on his part. Just as it says in, *John 15:13, "There is no greater love than to lay down one's life for one's friends."* Let me repeat that, but with a twist. "There is no greater love than to lay down one's life for one's stepchild."

Ironically, a few days after hearing about this situation, I heard a song by Randy Travis titled, "Raise Him Up[k]." I have heard the song before, but I suddenly realized that it painted a picture of Joseph as a stepfather. Part of the lyrics say,

> "Ya'll may have to look at Joseph,
> A couple thousand years ago.
> When he held a newborn baby he named Jesus.
> He said he may not be blood of my blood.
> Still I'm gonna raise him up."

He was blessed with the responsibility of raising, and nurturing Jesus. Joseph was strong enough to take on the job of stepdad, just as many stepfathers are today. What an example of laying down one's life for one's stepchild. He loved and nurtured Christ who became the sacrifice for our sins.

If there is a precious stepfather in your life, let him know God provided a role model for even him, because Joseph was the first real stepdad! Please tell him how much you love him today, pray a blessing over him and say Happy Father's Day—even if it isn't June!

ROCKS AND CHOCOLATES

Do you remember the movie *Forrest Gump*[1]? In the beginning of the movie, Forrest is handicapped and has braces on his legs. In spite of his learning disability and handicap, Mrs. Gump sends Forrest to the regular school. Forrest is a simple person who remembers the basic wisdom his Mama taught him. He is always able to look past the problems to the positive side of life. His Mama gave him the tools necessary to overcome his handicap. All too often we allow the problems of this world be our handicaps in life.

When they were growing up, Forrest and Jenny were best friends. There is a scene in the movie where Jenny returns home. Jenny and Forrest are walking and they come to the house where she grew up and was abused by her father. She begins showing her anger by throwing her shoes, and then rocks toward the house. She throws rocks until she falls to the ground. At that point Forrest says, "Sometimes, I guess there's just not enough rocks." Have you ever felt that way? Life can throw you one problem after another, and you just get tired of throwing rocks trying to solve the problems!

As I have grown in my Christian walk, I have learned to throw fewer rocks, and send up more prayers. But there are still so many times when I pick up that big rock, and give it a hard throw. As if to say, "Take that!" God has given us the ability to communicate with Him and so often we just don't do it. Our human nature is to take control of the situation, rather than giving God control. He is much more capable of making decisions than we are. Each of us occasionally needs to be reminded of *Ephesians 6:18a (NIV)*, *"Pray in the Spirit on all occasions with all kinds of prayers and requests."* The Bible teaches us to pray, and seek God's will for all our needs, not just the major problems.

Probably one of Forrest's most quoted phrases is, "My Mama always said, life was like a box of chocolates. You never know what you're gonna get." That statement is so true. We don't know what life holds, but the One who holds us does. While walking down the road of life, there are going to be many problems. Why not battle them with prayer, instead of rocks?

Matthew 18:20 (NIV) says, *"For where two or three come together in my name, there am I with them."* Take time today to find a friend, drop your rocks, open a box of chocolates, and spend some time in prayer. Let God help you through the problems of life, because it is definitely like a box of chocolates. "You never know what you're gonna get," but He does!

<u>Points to Ponder</u>

- What rocks in your life do you need to drop and turn into prayer today?
- Who do you know that would be your prayer partner?

DESTRUCTION LEADS TO CONSTRUCTION

Destruction—Demolition—Ruin—Damage—
Annihilation—Devastation

These are words we typically do not like to hear. They mean something has come to an end, like tossing out your favorite old jeans with the holes in them. Sometimes destruction is for the better, like when it leads to the construction of a new bridge.

- Grandma's china plate was demolished when I dropped it on the floor. It wasn't worth a lot, but I was devastated emotionally because Grandma was dear to my heart.
- My friendship was ruined because of some unkind words I said, they weren't meant to cause pain, but they did.
- My marriage has been damaged due to lies and deceit.

Have any of these words or similar words echoed through your mind at some point and time in your life? Unfortunately, I know they have mine.

Yet over time, I have come to realize that destruction eventually leads to construction. Sometimes God allows sentimental objects to be destroyed so we will cherish what is really important, the memories themselves, and not the material items.

Maybe God allowed a friendship to be hurt beyond repair for reasons we will never understand. Friends walk in and out of our lives constantly. Regardless of how the friendship was damaged, they may hold a special place in our hearts forever. The pain of separation can seem unbearable, almost like a divorce, but sometimes God says, "Let it go."

What about the devastation that can take place in marriage? Marriage is a give and take. It is falling in and out of love, over and over again with the same person. Unfortunately, there are occasions when the pain is too much to bear, and the decision is made to go separate ways. There are also times when construction begins, and reconciliation can be reached.

Recently the bridge in our neighborhood was demolished to build a new better bridge. The destruction took place in just a matter of days. However, the new bridge will be under construction for months. Is the physical bridge any different than the bridges of memories, friendship and marriage? They served their purpose at one time. They were destroyed quickly. They can be reconstructed over time. But the construction period takes work and time. They will become very different, and will be built on a new foundation.

During the past year, I have experienced the loss of a friendship. Though my heart would like to make amends, she does not have the same desire. But God has put before me a new friend. One who is much like myself. We share the same passion for serving the Lord. We talk about our strong willed adult children, and we are building a God centered friendship. Ironically, she has helped bring healing to my broken heart, and understanding to a situation I have struggled with for months. In my situation, God says, "Let it go, but turn this direction to build a new friendship."

I also have walked the road of divorce. I married young, we had our differences, and it did not end like all our young dreams portrayed. It seems so many years ago, though today I can say we are friends because we have a common bond of two sons. Amid the destruction of a marriage, God constructed something new for the benefit of our children. We have set our differences aside for the two most important people in our lives. We have both remarried, and our children now have four parents instead of two, who love them very much. God constructed a different relationship between us, but it provides a bridge to our children.

I know God will use every broken part of my life to help someone else who travels a similar road. I have walked beside many friends who have struggled through marital problems, and sometimes divorce. God has called me to use my experiences to help them through their similar struggles. One day I am sure He will use my broken friendship to come alongside someone who is feeling the same pain which I have experienced.

In the mean time, God and I are in the construction business. I am building relationships and mending bridges where possible. God is the architect and builder of my new bridges. I am just laying the foundation and pavement along the way. He gives me the strength, and ability to do so because, *1 Corinthians 10:13 (MSG)* says, *"No test or temptation that comes your way is beyond the course of what others have had to face. All you need to remember is that God will never let you down; he'll never let you be pushed past your limit; he'll always be there to help you come through it."*

<u>Points to Ponder</u>

- Is there a bridge in your life you need to mend, or does it need a total reconstruction?
- Is your pain causing you or someone else to suffer? If so, ask God to help you mend the relationship and build a new bridge.
- God may be saying, "Let it go." If so, ask God to help you do so through prayer, as you let go today.

Rose Among Thorns

Jesus tells the Parable of the Sower to a large crowd, which can be found in the gospels of *Matthew, Mark* and *Luke*. His story is of a farmer who is sowing seed. Some seed falls along the path, and is trampled. Other seed falls on the rocks, and when it comes up it withers due to the lack of moisture. Some of the seed falls among the thorns, and the thorns choke out the plants. But other seed falls on good soil, and yields a much larger crop than the seeds which were sewn.

The disciples did not always understand Jesus' parables, and asked Him to explain the meaning of each example of seed. The seed along the path represents those who hear the Word, but Satan prevents them from believing, and being saved. The seed among the rocks is an example of those who hear the Word, but it doesn't take root in their lives. As soon as troubles come their way, they no longer believe. The seed which is sewn among the thorns represents those who let life's worries and troubles take over, and they never mature as Christians. The seed which falls on the good soil is wonderfully described in *Luke 8:15 (NIV)*. *"But the seed on good soil stands for those with a noble and good heart, who hear the word, retain it, and by persevering produce a crop."*

I recently became acquainted with a young Christian lady whose walk with Christ is a living example of this verse. Terri grew up in foster care, living in numerous homes during her childhood. But out of many of those homes, there were seeds planted in her life by some of the families she encountered along the way. She could have easily become discouraged with life, and have represented the seed sewn along the path which is trampled, or the seed in the rocks and thorns. But Terri didn't allow this to happen. The seeds which were planted in her heart at a young age were planted in good soil. They sprouted, grew and continue to multiply daily.

I told Terri that she is a rose among thorns, as God has planted her in many challenging situations in her life. She is surrounded by unbelievers whom she dearly loves, and she doesn't give up. She continues to sow seeds of love and compassion, yet learns to set Christian boundaries for her family so she can stay firmly grounded in the Word. Her prayer is that one day the seeds she is sewing will fall on good soil as they did in her life.

God laid out the plan for Terri's life long before she was ever born. He knew the path which she would travel, and knit her together in a perfect plan, a plan for her to be a witness to others among the thorns of life *(Psalm 139:13–14)*. He gave her the strength, courage, and personality necessary to persevere in sharing God's love to those in need.

Not only is she a witness to those who don't know Christ, but she is a witness to me, and everyone to whom she shares her story. I grew up in a Christian home, and have never had to face the struggles and trials in life she has faced. It does my soul good to know that the small problems I face in life can easily be overcome with faith and prayer as she is a living example of the true meaning of perseverance.

Points to Ponder

* Read one of the references to the Parable of the Sower. *Matthew 13:1–23, Mark 4:1–20, Luke 8:4–15*

- Where are you in your spiritual walk? Is God's Word falling along the path, on the stones, among the thorns, or is it taking root in your life?
- Is there someone in your life who needs to see God's love and compassion through you?
- Are you persevering to reach them?

CLEAN YOUR CLOSET

It is spring, and sometimes that motivates me to do some extra cleaning. I have recently cleaned a couple of closets which were neglected for a very long time. It isn't a fun job, but sometimes it is necessary. Today I tackled my husband's closet where he stores all of his work clothes for the farm. Oh the treasures (or should I say trash) I found. Old hats and shoes. New hats and mismatched gloves. More old hats and broken suspenders. Hunting caps and worn out jeans. Collectable hats and shoe insoles. Dirt and dust bunnies and numerous coats. Oh, did I forget to mention hats! Every farmer I know owns way too many hats, and his wife will agree.

To truly clean the closet it would have required a huge trash can, but instead I sorted many items for further use. Eventually a mate was found for every glove and you never know when you might need a pair of broken suspenders to fix another pair. Right? I organized many items into bags, baskets and boxes and returned them to the closet. Why did I do that? I cleaned the closet like many of us clean our spiritual closets. We hold onto that one item of sin from the past, or our worries and stress. Instead we need to give them all to the Lord. It isn't a fun job to clean your spiritual closet, but often it is necessary for our spiritual growth!

We all have dirt and dust bunnies in our lives. They are referred to by one little word called sin. *Romans 3:23 (NIV)* tells us, *"For all have sinned and fall short of the glory of God."* But it is our job to get out the broom and ask God to sweep away our sins daily. What about the old shoes and boots in your closet? Maybe you have used your words or actions to trample someone recently. God requires us to choose our words wisely and to show compassion on one another with our lips. *"Pleasant words are a honeycomb, sweet to the soul, and healing to the bones" (Proverbs 16:24 NASB).*

Worn out jeans and broken suspenders. Do you just feel like your life is worn out or broken right now? Maybe you are absolutely tired, to the point of exhaustion from the stress in your life. Rest in God's presence and allow Him to heal your broken spirit. Just sit before Him and feel His presence. You may have no words to speak, but that is okay, because He knows your heart and your pain. One of my favorite verses which reminds me God is always present, and always cares is *Psalm 46:10, "Be still, and know that I am God!"*

Similar to all the hats in the closet, what in your life do you have too much of? Maybe your old hats represent gossip or evil thoughts? Or is it your temper or lack of respect for others? Are your new hats stress and worry due to a recent change in your life? Instead of repeating these sins over and over again, allow God to build the fruits of the spirit in your life. Look for opportunities to show *"Love, joy, peace, patience, kindness, goodness, faithfulness, gentleness, and self-control (Galatians 5:22–23)."*

Are you busy seeking worldly success, money or material items, and have very little time for God? Take off your hunting cap, and set aside your worldly desires. *Matthew 6:25, 27* tells us, *"That is why I tell you not to worry about everyday life—whether you have enough food and drink, or enough clothes to wear. Isn't life more than food, and your body more than clothing? Can all your worries add a single moment to your life?"* Simply hunt for God in the blessed life He has already given you!

When we clean our spiritual closet God asks us not to keep a single item. He asks that we have enough faith to lay down our worries, our sins, our past, our present, and our future at the foot of the cross. Our closets are overflowing from life. Sometimes we can't even shut the door. Sit before Christ today and take everything to Him at the foot of the cross. When doing so, we are forgiven, renewed, and blessed. As you clean your spiritual closet today, meditate on the words of *Matthew 11:28–30* as they are beautifully written in The Message.

> *"Are you tired? Worn out? Burned out on religion? Come to me. Get away with me and you'll recover your life. I'll show you how to take a real rest. Walk with me and work with me—watch how I do it. Learn the unforced rhythms of grace. I won't lay anything heavy or ill-fitting on you. Keep company with me and you'll learn to live freely and lightly."*

Vacation Dud

Whenever we vacation we usually have one stop, or one incident that is the dud of the trip. My family likes to joke with me about whale watching. There was the time that I insisted on a side trip to see the whales. The guide pointed to a whale floating off in the far distance. It looked more like a large blob than it did a whale, so of course they frequently tease me about the time Mom forced everyone to go whale watching, I mean blob watching.

We have had hotel incidents, like the time we laid down for the night and prayed that there were no weird creepy, crawly critters running around while we caught a couple of winks. The four of us left the next morning shivering, and we chuckle every time we reminisce. On another incident we left before the creepy, crawly critters had a chance to crawl. We politely left them a twenty dollar cleaning fee after being in the room for about thirty minutes. The entire time we were there, sweat beads were forming from the lack of air conditioning in the room. If you want to get a chuckle out of anyone in our family, all you have to say is, "Dis not good! Dis not good!" Those were the last words spoken by an upset hotel owner's wife. Even though her husband agreed on the amount needed to clean the room, she apparently felt differently.

This year's dud was a scenic railroad trip. It was scenic if you like looking at overgrown shrubs, briars and a dried up river. Maybe earlier in the summer, or perhaps when fall colors are vibrant it would be a scenic ride, but the river gorge had little to offer us in the way of beauty in late August.

Much like vacation duds, I have experienced what I felt were ministry duds. I helped plan an event for one hundred and fifty attendees, and we barely broke forty. I will spend the next five years using up the leftover table favors and gift bags. Or I have lead Bible Study groups where I just don't feel like I am making a difference. I study, prepare, ask questions, but they just don't seem to talk or open up to the lessons. I struggle, thinking I'm just not a good leader. But, at the same time, I am sure God called me to lead the studies.

It is our human nature to compare ourselves to past success, another's success, or just the grand plan in our own mind. When we do this, we never stack up! We always want more success, more people attending, or better results. But what does Christ want from us in these circumstances? God wants us to give it our best, but His best is very different from ours. If a Bible study or event doesn't go the way we plan, we aren't a failure in God's eyes. God considers all we do to reach the lost a success. There are times when a small event is better, and much more intimate. The quiet Bible Study may simply be a sign of God working in the lives of those attending as they absorb every truth from God's Word. God has a greater plan in everything we do. We simply have to look at His plan, and not our own. We need to make ourselves available to serve as it says in *2 Timothy*.

> *Do your best to present yourself to God as one approved, a worker who does not need to be ashamed and who correctly handles the word of truth. (2 Timothy 2:15 NIV)*

> *In the presence of God and of Christ Jesus who will judge the living and the dead, and in view of his appearing and his kingdom, I give you this charge: Preach the*

Word; be prepared in season and out of season; correct,
rebuke and encourage—with great patience and
careful instruction. (2 Timothy 4:1–2 NIV)

A vacation dud doesn't ruin a trip, it creates a memory which is what vacationing is all about. We need to allow our ministry duds to be evaluated in God's eyes, and except them as memories as well. There are no ministry duds when you present yourself to Christ as a servant. Take time to follow Christ, and be prepared for all the ministry He guides you through. Continue with patience as you serve, knowing that God does not compare by numbers, or by words spoken, but by the loyalty with which you serve.

PRECIOUS CARGO

Two days a week I babysit my granddaughter Mya. Most days we stay home and play, but we do take the occasional trip. On a trip to Great Grandma Conklin's house this week, I noticed that driving with Mya in the car was much different. I took all the extra precautionary steps. There are no rolling stops, which are very common on back country roads. Always complete stops and looking both ways. Okay—maybe three times at a busy intersection. Doing the speed limit or under like a puttering grandma is a must. No need to change the radio station, or fiddle with buttons either. Why all the extra precautions? Because Mya is precious cargo! If something would happen to her, I would be devastated.

The day after our trip to Great Grandma's house, I was running errands. I had a lot to accomplish and a short time to accomplish it. I was in such a hurry trying to squeeze everything in my day. I drove a little over the speed limit, did the occasional rolling stop and looked quickly at intersections. I fiddled with the radio buttons to find my favorite songs. I had already returned to all my careless driving habits instead of learning from the day before. Suddenly it dawned on me. Why am I acting like this? In God's eyes, I am precious cargo too. And what about the people in the other vehicles or pedestrians I might pass? If I am driving carelessly, what message am I sending them? They are just as precious to God as Mya is to me.

God loves each of us so much that He sent his only son, Jesus, to die on the cross for us *(John 3:16)*. He loves you and me just as much as I love Mya. *Romans 8:37–39ᵐ* paints a beautiful picture of His love for us.

> *But in all these things we are completely victorious*
> *through God who showed his love for us. Yes, I am*
> *sure that neither death, nor life, nor angels, nor ruling*
> *spirits, nothing now, nothing in the future, no powers,*
> *nothing above us, nothing below us, nor anything else*
> *in the whole world will ever be able to separate us from*
> *the love of God that is in Christ Jesus our Lord.*

We are all such precious cargo to Christ, yet we rush through life with just the opposite attitude. It is so much more than bad driving habits or road rage. We treat one another with disrespect, gossip, hate and jealousy, just to name a few. We don't take time to lend a hand, call a friend, or pray for one another. Yet Christ forgives us for all our wrongs, and loves us regardless of our flaws. Reread verse 39 again, *"Nothing above us, nothing below us, nor anything else in the whole world will ever be able to separate us from the love of God that is in Christ Jesus our Lord."* Do you hear that message of love? Nothing you have done or will do, can stop God from loving you! What an example of forgiveness and unconditional love! When we grasp the concept that He died for us, and He loves us no matter what, life changes.

As you pray over these verses today ask God to show you His unconditional love, and let you feel the power of being treated like His precious cargo. When you take your next road trip, leave a few minutes early and drive like you and others are precious cargo, because you are loved and they are loved. Yes, we are all loved by the King!

COMMITMENT

It seems to me that commitment is a word that is taken lightly in our society today. Just as an example, you can see a lack of commitment to marriage and family, hard work, and the church.

Yet as human beings, God puts within us a passion, and when we find passion for something we love, we become totally committed. In some cases it might be a sports team, or a medical research cause such as breast cancer. There are many ways to be committed, and serve the Lord outside of church, but what about within the church as well. Sadly, within churches there is often a lack of commitment. We need to become so in love with Jesus, that we are committed to help with ministry, attend various functions where we learn and grow, and bring others to Christ.

Let's look at a few familiar verses below, where true commitment comes from the basics. These basics are taking time to study God's Word, and applying it to our lives. When we look at commitment from this biblical standpoint, it is something God requests of us. In *Psalm 37:5* we learn, *"Commit everything you do to the Lord. Trust him, and he will help you."* *Proverbs 16:3* tells us when we commit, we will be successful. *"Commit your actions to the Lord, and your plans will succeed."*

But how do we accomplish this? How do we learn to trust Him so whole heartedly that we will walk by faith knowing that our plans will succeed? I believe the clue is *Proverbs 23:12 "Commit yourself to instruction; listen carefully to words of knowledge."* It is digging into

God's word, knowing His will, learning His truths, that sets us on a course for true commitment in all we do. We have to be willing to go the extra mile. Run the race. Get back up when we are knocked down. And continually seek answers from God's Word. When we do this, we will find true commitment to Christ, and to His church.

I was recently touched by a powerful musical rendition of "The Lord's Prayer". We find these common words in *Matthew 6:9–13 (KJV)*. Often times it is the first prayer we commit to memory, or teach our children. In many denominations it is said frequently during services. If we truly listen to the words spoken by Jesus, He is instructing us to be totally committed to God for everything! As you read these verses, think of your own life, and your commitment. Do you walk each day asking that God's will be done? Do you rely on God for your daily nourishment? Do you recognize the fact that God truly has all the power and glory, but it is your choice to make a total commitment to Him daily? As you pray this prayer, think of the true meaning of each sentence. Commit yourself to Christ, and the growth of His church today.

Our Father which art in heaven, Hallowed be thy name.
Thy kingdom come, Thy will be done in earth, as it is in heaven.
Give us this day our daily bread.
And forgive us our debts, as we forgive our debtors.
And lead us not into temptation, but deliver us from evil:
For thine is the kingdom, and the power, and the glory, forever.
Amen.

LITTLE THINGS

Sometimes life just gets a little discouraging. From small troubles to the big ones it just begins to weigh us down. My husband and I have said numerous times that we thought life would get easier as we grew older, but it seems like it has gotten harder. Maybe the decisions we are making are more major, and the problems we face from time to time are more heartbreaking.

In spite of the daily grind of life, we still try to find a bright spot each day. Some little perk or pick me up to put a smile on our faces. For Jim this week it came from our granddaughter Mya. With the innocence of a two and a half year old, she walked up to Grandpa with those big blue eyes and said, "I love you Papaw." Talk about melting his heart and making his day. It made his year!

For me last week it was a happy face. I was puttering around the kitchen at some odd jobs and pouting over numerous, minor problems. I opened a jar of honey to fill the honey bear and there was my sign from heaven. God gave me a happy face on the lid of the honey jar. A sticky, gooey happy face! I couldn't help but smile in spite of everything on my mind. After all, how many times have you opened a jar and received a smile. It was a message saying, "Cheer up. Be happy. I have it under control. All is well."

Was the Samaritan woman at the well saying, "All is well" in her world before she met Jesus? Doubting Thomas wasn't singing a happy tune after his Rabbi had been crucified. All was definitely not well for the woman who was about to be stoned for committing adultery! And what about the woman who had been bleeding for twelve years and was considered unclean. Did she feel as if all was well in her world?

The Bible gives examples of many people who were troubled in their soul. They were bitter, hurt, sinful, despised, unworthy, doubting, rejected people. But then along comes Jesus, and He made everything better!

To the Samaritan woman Christ said, *"I AM the Messiah!" (John 4:26).* Thomas was told, *"Put your finger here, and look at my hands. Put your hand into the wound in my side. Don't be faithless any longer. Believe!" (John 20:27).* Jesus spoke to the adulterous woman saying, *"Where are your accusers? Didn't even one of them condemn you?... Neither do I. Go and sin no more" (John 8:10–11).* To the woman with an issue of blood Jesus said, *"Daughter, be encouraged! Your faith has made you well" (Matthew 9:22).* But to us, Christ says it all! We have the scriptures to tell us that He is the Messiah. He was crucified, dead and buried, and rose again. We have examples of faith and a Father who loves us unconditionally, just like the unconditional love of a child.

I don't know what might be troubling your soul today, but please remember that you have the great I Am with you. Always remember to look for the little perks in life, such as a hug from a loved one, a scripture that touches your heart, or a favorite song. It could be the innocence of a child, or maybe even a happy face on a jar lid. I believe that during those moments of turmoil and discouragement, God will send you a sign to brighten your day. And as the old hymn, "It Is Well with My Soul[n]" says,

> "When peace like a river attendeth my way,
> When sorrows like sea-billows roll;
> Whatever my lot, Thou hast taught me to say,
> 'It is well, it is well with my soul.'"

Suggested Scripture Reading

- *John 4:1–38*
- *John 20:24–29*
- *John 8:1–11*
- *Matthew 9:20–22*
- *Hebrews 11*

My Happy Face

Volunteer Violas

A couple of years ago I had a few volunteer violas pop up in a flowerbed. The previous year I had planted violas in the flowerpots on the front porch and in their exuberance to volunteer and reproduce, they came up where I didn't want them to grow. I didn't have the heart to just kill the flowers, so I transplanted them to the back of the house. They weren't really planted in a flowerbed, but in hard soil near some pine trees. I decided if they grew, fine. If not, no big deal. I really didn't water them often or even worry about them. Now two years later, they are a beauty to behold! Those three or four small plants have multiplied into a small forest of purple and yellow beauty this spring. They are so beautiful that I purchased more violas, and planted them alongside the sidewalk which leads to our deck. Unlike the volunteers, these plants were planted in good soil. If the volunteers can multiply in bad soil, what beauty I will see next spring in the good soil! Hopefully in the near future the two will grow and connect to one another, and cover the entire area.

How do you grow volunteers in your church or ministry? Do you plant a volunteer in a ministry field that has bad soil, and hope they grow? Or do you come alongside them and work together until they have blossomed? There is such a need for volunteers within churches, and ministries that many times we plant volunteers where they cannot flourish. If a volunteer does not have a gift which will make them a good teacher, please don't ask them to teach. God has given each of us gifts and talents, and when we use them together, we become the body of Christ. Unlike my violas planted in the hard soil, many volunteers planted in hard soil fade away because they don't have the proper skills or training to bloom where they are planted.

This year three of us have teamed together to lead the prayer ministry in our church. We are fortunate to have many volunteers who pray during the services on Sunday mornings. Our goal is to eventually unite two people in prayer during each service. *"For where two or three gather together as my followers, I am there among them"* (Matthew 18:20).

One Sunday a friend approached my husband after the service, and asked if he had been praying during the service. Her eyes filled with tears when he confirmed that, yes, he had been praying for everyone in the service, which included her. The following week, I asked if she would like to join me in the prayer room some Sunday. After a short explanation of how I approach the prayer time, she agreed. On Sunday, as we began to pray, Dee's eyes filled with tears once again as she prayed, "Lord this is another big step for me, to be here listening to You and praying for others." We each prayed aloud and then went into silent prayer during most of the service. As the service came to an end, I had focused on one of the scriptures from the sermon. *James 3:13, "If you are wise and understand God's ways, prove it by living an honorable life, doing good works with the humility that comes from wisdom."* Dee and I made that our closing prayer. We didn't have the wisdom to know what to pray on Sunday morning, but we had the wisdom to know that prayer makes a difference. We had humbled ourselves to pray for others, and allowed the Holy Spirit to work through us.

Just before Dee and I parted ways, with tears in her eyes she said, "It was so different to be in here praying during the service rather than being in the sanctuary." And for me, it was so wonderful to pray together knowing that where two are gathered together, the Holy Spirit is among them. As a leader in the Prayer Ministry, I came alongside a volunteer. Hopefully she left that day with her roots planted in good soil from the experience. My hope and prayer is that Dee will reflect on her experience, and the gifts God has given her. Dee has a heart for helping others, and I pray she will continue to volunteer in the prayer room. As we come alongside one another, the ministry will continue to grow so others will witness the power of prayer.

I challenge you to not only use your gifts where God plants you, but to use them humbly, doing good works with the wisdom God has blessed upon you.

SQUIRREL OR OPOSSUM

Have you ever noticed the difference in animals as you are closely approaching them in a car? There is the squirrel. He scurries back and forth in front of you trying to decide which way to go. He just has this appearance of panic and frustration being unable to make a decision.

Then, there is the opossum. As you approach in your car, he lies down and acts as if he is dead. Though he thinks he is being clever, how risky is that maneuver! He just gives up and uses the only defense he knows which is no defense at all.

Many times in our Christian life, we are exactly like the squirrel and the opossum. We are so busy helping with church events, teaching Sunday School, singing in the choir, and serving on church committees that we act like the squirrel. We are constantly rushing from one event to the next, zigzagging through life. Or maybe you are more like the opossum, when someone comes your way looking for volunteers, you play dead. You are secretly hoping they will ask one of the squirrels. After all they have all the energy.

Maybe you are a little bit of both. You have been the squirrel zigzagging for months, and have reached total exhaustion. You are now suffering from what is commonly known as church burnout. This has led you to become an opossum. You are just going to play dead for awhile, and let someone else pick up the slack.

God's desire for us is somewhere in the middle. He would like us to be more like my border collie, Bailey. Bailey has a talent for running and retrieving. If you throw a pop bottle or a stick, she will bring it back with great speed and accuracy. But when hot and tired, she finds rest in a swimming pool. She rejuvenates herself before retrieving again. Bailey uses her talents and abilities to achieve a purpose, and her pool for rest.

Sometimes Bailey wants our attention when we are too busy to play. She will continually drop her toy at our feet, until we finally give it a toss. Isn't this a little bit like God? He will continue to nudge us, until we pay attention. Like Bailey, God wants nothing more than a relationship with us. He wants us to take time out of our busy lives to be with Him.

According to *Romans 12:6*, we are each given different gifts to do certain things well. God expects us to know our spiritual gifts, and use them to further His kingdom. He also desires a relationship with us. He doesn't want us to go through life zigzagging like a squirrel.

> *"Come to me, all you who are weary and burdened, and I will give you rest. Take my yoke upon you and learn from me, for I am gentle and humble in heart, and you will find rest for your souls." (Matthew 11:28– 29 NIV)*

God doesn't expect you to bear the burden of Christian work alone. He wants to be yoked with you where you will learn and find rest.

He promises to refresh us in *Jeremiah 31:25 (NIV), "I will refresh the weary and satisfy the faint."* Our goal as Christians is to live a balanced life. We are to live our lives like Bailey, somewhere in between the squirrel and the opossum. My prayer for you today is that you not only use your talents for Christ, but that you listen to Him, and find rest in a pool of love and compassion at his feet.

Suggested Scripture Reading

- Look up the word weary in the concordance of your Bible and see the examples of God providing rest.
- *Romans 12:6*

$\mathcal{B}$OX OF MEMORIES

I have a box which contains many memories from my past. I have a crown from when I was the Ostrander 4th of July Queen as a teenager, and pictures from high school days. In the closet is a saxophone which I haven't played in years, but it is a symbol of great memories for me. My husband has a box of wrestling posters, trophies and his BV letter from high school. These are all great memories and part of our lives. Memories which shaped us into the people we are today.

I have other special memories as well, like accepting Christ as my Savior as a teenager, and being immersed in baptism as an adult. And marrying Jim and growing together through difficult times and good times. We also have memories we would like to forget, but should we? Each and every part of our lives is a stepping stone as God molds us, and builds our faith story.

One such memory for me is when Jim was seriously ill in the hospital. On Friday night he had chills which couldn't be controlled. On Saturday he was told he had an infection in his leg, and was prescribed antibiotics. By Sunday I was sitting in the hospital room as heart monitors and IVs were being administered to him. One doctor was telling me the infection in his leg was very serious, while another was telling me his heart was beating out of sinus rhythm. In the weeks and months to come, Jim was in and out the hospital twice for the infection. He had to return to the hospital three times a day for eight weeks for IV antibiotics. Then after the infection was cured, there were even more hospital visits as they attempted to return his heart to sinus rhythm.

What a painful memory. So why would God ask me to reflect on such a difficult time in our lives? On that horrible Sunday, God was with me in the hospital room. I felt very alone as Jim rested with a very high fever. I had recently heard the gospel song titled, "Praise His Name°" and I began to sing the chorus as I prayed.

> "When it seems you're all alone
> Praise His name
> When you feel you can't go on
> Just raise your hands and say
> Greater is He that is within me
> You can praise the hurt away
> If you'll just praise his name"

While praying the chorus on Sunday afternoon, I felt a peace come over me as God spoke to my spirit and said Jim would be okay. This song became my prayer over the next twenty-four hours, and it was very comforting to me in the weeks which followed. During this time, a huge support group of friends and family came to help drive Jim to the hospital three times a day, and provide meals, so I could return to work.

God asks us to take our memories out of the box and share them. Some are tools which mold us into the person we have become. Others are to be used as a witness to glorify Christ.

Where would we be today if some of the great examples of faith had put their memories in a box and never shared what God did for them? *Hebrews 11* tells us that Noah built an ark to save his family from things not yet seen. The Israelites celebrated the Passover every year. It was a reminder of God passing over their homes, and saving their first born during the plague in Egypt. This plague ultimately softened Pharaoh's heart, and led to their release from slavery *(Exodus 12)*. The gospel tells us of Lazarus being raised from the dead *(John 11:1–44)*. These and countless other stories were shared as examples of faith, and how God touched their lives, so we could believe many, many years later.

God has given each of us a faith story to share, and He calls us to witness to others. Jim's stay in the hospital is merely a chapter in my life which I can share and say, "God is a great Comforter and Healer in times of need." What about you? What memories do you have tucked away in a box? Don't be too scared to remove the lid off of your box, and let others know what God has done in your life. God wastes nothing! He uses the good and bad memories to glorify His Kingdom. Please reflect on the words of *Philemon verse 6 (NIV)*. *"I pray that you may be active in sharing your faith, so that you will have a full understanding of every good thing we have in Christ."* Starting today, open your box of faith stories, and use them as examples of what Jesus Christ has done for you.

DOILIES AND CHINA

Recently my mother gave me several doilies and lace table clothes. All of them came from my sister-in-law who recently passed away. I also have the china which came from my Grandma. Though I cherish the memories of these ladies and the fact that these keepsakes were theirs, I will seldom use them. I will keep them for their sentimental value. The china displays in my china cupboard and gets used once in a while. The doilies and lace are tucked away in a drawer for safe keeping. Is this wrong of me? My Mom and I just have very different decorating styles. At my Mom's house, when it is time for a big family dinner like Thanksgiving, all the doilies and lace come out and the table is adorned with china. I on the other hand am a simple person, who is more likely to pull out a placemat made of denim and hand you a plastic dinner plate, simply because it is less work! Neither one of us is wrong. We just have our own styles.

When I think about tucking away these keepsakes, I think about how this relates to tucking Jesus away in my heart. I can keep Him to myself, or I can tell others about Christ. In *John 21:17b* Christ said to Peter, *"Feed my sheep."* This doesn't mean to toss a few sheep some grass and oats, it means spread the news of Christ's death and resurrection. In *Mark 16:15–18* we read of the great commission. This passage begins with, *"Go into all the world and preach the Good News to everyone."* In other words, feeding His sheep by telling everyone about Christ!

God has blessed me with many stories which I can share with others that might deepen their faith. I can share how my sister-in-law Pat endured much pain and suffering in her lifetime, yet she held strong to her faith in God. There were times when I remember her saying that she was mad at God for all the suffering. In spite of this, she would always come back and find peace in Him. I understood why she was mad at times. During her lifetime, she endured the loss of two children, and a house fire which destroyed everything. She also endured a horrible automobile accident, which caused her to have arthritis later in life, along with the pain and suffering which accompanies the disease. Through it all her faith may have wavered at times, but she never lost sight of God. She held tight to Christ through many difficulties.

My Grandma Conklin taught me to have a quiet time with Jesus daily, as she read her Bible every night before she went to bed. She instilled in me at a very young age the importance of reading God's Word. She invested in my life by giving of her time, and showing me how much she cared. When I went through my divorce, Grandma was one of the first to show forgiveness by not judging me. She didn't ask questions or ask for reasons why the marriage failed. She simply told me that she loved me.

Both of these godly women have gone on to be with the Lord, but I am still here, and can be their voice and tell their stories. If I come across someone who has suffered like Pat, I can share her story of endurance, questioning God, and holding strong to her faith. If I can teach someone the importance of reading the Bible by sharing Grandma's story, I am helping to feed God's sheep. Showing forgiveness and not judgment is a trait which may lead someone closer to Christ, and the ultimate gift of salvation. What a blessing to have their examples of how to fulfill the great commission, by just being godly women. When I look at my roots, these two wonderful ladies are just a couple of the people who have touched my life. Now it is my turn to reach out to others and do the same.

I don't know what the future holds for me, or who will cross my path. I do have faith that God will continue to use their stories and examples of faith as long as I continue to feed His sheep. I know my memories of them will fade, but the hope they found in the Lord can live on forever. After all, if I feel their memory slipping away, I can always put out the doilies, lace table clothes, and china for dinner one night. I hope they will always serve as a reminder for me to share the Good News with everyone God sends my way.

$\mathcal{H}$ONEST MISTAKE

Sometimes God truly works in mysterious ways. My typical process throughout writing this book is to do the following: Write the devotion. My friend Angie and wonderful hubby, Jim, read it and offer any suggestions they may have. A few days or weeks later, I reread the devotion and make any necessary changes. I then email it to my friend Rachel who proofreads it for grammar issues and other suggestions. I make any changes once again, and consider the document ready. The prior devotion in this book, "Doilies and China" was no different. After a few weeks of going through these steps, the devotion was in the final stage. I was reading it for the last time when I said, "Oh no! The china was not my Grandma's china! " It was an honest mistake. I was probably on a roll writing that day and wasn't thinking clearly. The china was actually my Great Aunt Peg's passed down through my Grandma. I don't even remember Aunt Peg, so a simple change from Grandma to Aunt Peg was not going to correct the problem. For days and days all I could think was, "What do I do about this devotion? Do I just eliminate it? Didn't God give me the message for a reason?"

Of course I asked my faithful supporters for their honest opinion and received different answers. I kept thinking about their suggestions and praying. I truly felt God had put the message of "Doilies and China" on my heart, so omitting it just didn't make any sense. I tried changing the china to some of Grandma's other items, but they just didn't fit the story and it lost all meaning. Since no immediate solution came to me, I just focused on other aspects of the book.

Today I found my answer as I was reading the book, *Successful Women Think Differently* by Valorie Burton[P]. In the beginning of the book Valorie asks the reader to commit to seven key decisions. Decision #3 just happens to be, "I choose to be authentic." My decision at that point seemed so easy. Leave the devotion as is, but be authentic with my readers. It was an honest mistake. As I thought about other devotions, I realized that each story from my childhood or life may or may not be totally accurate. But they are how I remember them. My memories could be slightly different from what other family members experienced. I may see a different side of a story or person, but when you are authentic before God, He uses everything for His glory.

God shows us grace for both our big sins and our honest mistakes. When I looked for synonyms of the word grace I found the words favor and mercy. We can't begin to fathom the depth of God's grace and mercy. In *Psalm 4:1* David prayed, *"Have mercy on me and hear my prayer."* In *Psalm 28:6* David had the opposite response, *"Praise the Lord! For he has heard my cry for mercy."* We not only need to seek God's grace and mercy, but we need to thank Him for it!

Am I worried that God won't forgive an honest mistake? Absolutely not. It led me to do a little more Bible reading on the subject of grace, and I am always thankful for tidbits of knowledge in God's Word. *Genesis 6:8, 1 Samuel 2:26*, and *Luke 1:30* all reassure us that we can find favor in the Lord. *"Noah found favor with the Lord." "Samuel…grew in favor with the Lord."* And *"Mary…you have found favor in the Lord."* I love this familiar scripture which you can turn into a prayer for your loved ones. It is *Numbers 6:25–27, "May the Lord smile on you and be gracious to you. May the Lord show you his favor and give you his peace."*

So as I confess my honest mistake to you and the Lord, I know He will extend a hand of grace to me, and find favor in me for being an authentic Christian. I will never look at Grandma's china quite the same. Grandma taught me to spend time in God's Word, and today I have enjoyed reading many scriptures about grace, favor and mercy. The best tidbit I found to share with you today is one that Grandma would have loved.

> *When God our Savior revealed his kindness and love, he saved us, not because of the righteous things we had done, but because of his mercy. He washed away our sins, giving us a new birth and new life through the Holy Spirit. He generously poured out the Spirit upon us through Jesus Christ our Savior. (Titus 3:4–6)*

Dear Lord, please smile on my friends, family and the readers of this devotion. Be gracious to them and show them Your favor and Your peace today. May You shine upon them as they grow closer to You each day and learn more of Your amazing grace and mercy. Amen

Suggested Scripture Reading

- *Psalm 31:22*
- *Psalm 41:4*
- *Psalm 51:1*
- *Proverbs 3:3–4*
- *Luke 2:39–40*
- *1 Corinthians 15:9–10*
- Take a few moments to look up the words grace, favor, and mercy in your concordance and meditate on a few favorite verses of your own.

A Time

"It is enough Lord!" Did you ever have one of those days or weeks when you cry out to God with those words? Well this week was one of those weeks. It started with terrible news that a very close friend was diagnosed with fast growing breast cancer at a young age of thirty-nine. It was then followed by the tragic death of a young mother, who was only thirty years old. Shortly following childbirth she became ill, and left behind two children under the age of two. In the midst of this shock, I received word that my friend's mom had finally lost her very long battle with cancer. Yes—it definitely was enough for one week.

My husband and I attended the graveside services for my friend's mother. As the pastor was speaking of Shirley's life, I listened intently to the type of person she was to her friends and family. He made comments like: Known for her cookies. Always thought of others first. Beloved wife of fifty-three years. At peace with God. It became obvious to me that she lived life to the fullest, and I hope these thoughts will one day comfort the family again.

Amid the many people at the cemetery was a small child, probably about one year old. Like most children that age, she was pacifying her time by toddling around behind the crowd. As I watched this child, I saw joy and it was comforting. She was unaware of the sadness around her.

As the pastor spoke of Shirley's wish for a memorial flower garden to be created, this little toddler started picking dandelions from the yard. I found the situation to be such a God moment, yet a little bit ironic. As many adults were grieving, the child was smiling. Our thoughts were being directed toward a memorial flower garden, and she picked dandelions, and handed them to her father. Oh the beauty of seeing life though the eyes of a child.

As I read my devotions the following morning they included *Ecclesiastes 3:1–8*[q].

> *To everything there is a season,*
> *A time for every purpose under heaven:*
> *A time to be born, And a time to die;*
> *A time to plant, And a time to pluck what is planted;*
> *A time to kill, And a time to heal;*
> *A time to break down, And a time to build up;*
> *A time to weep, And a time to laugh;*
> *A time to mourn, And a time to dance;*
> *A time to cast away stones, And a time to gather stones;*
> *A time to embrace, And a time to refrain from embracing;*
> *A time to gain, And a time to lose;*
> *A time to keep, And a time to throw away;*
> *A time to tear, And a time to sew;*
> *A time to keep silence, And a time to speak;*
> *A time to love, And a time to hate;*
> *A time of war, And a time of peace.*

What comforting words to my soul following such a sad week. For those attending the funeral yesterday, it was a time to weep and a time to mourn. To a child, it was a time to laugh and a time to dance. May we never forget in the midst of our sorrow, to return to the memories where we can recall times of laughter and times of dancing. Even though our loved ones are desperately missed, we have the pleasure of knowing we will one day be reunited.

May we also remember there is a time for all emotions, but God is the Almighty Comforter. In the days to come I will continue to pray for my friend who lost his daughter during childbirth. I will pray for my friend who is battling cancer, and pray for my friend and her family who are grieving the loss of a loved one.

THE FLAME

Before you start to read this devotion, take time to light a candle and relax. Study the flame for a few moments as it slowly moves about in the air. Maybe your candle is scented. If so, take a few deep breaths, relax, and enjoy the smell as it fills the air. We live in such a busy world, and we seldom take the time to truly unwind, and focus our minds on Christ. I struggle in this area, and feel that I'm giving up control if I allow myself to lose focus for even a few moments.

This week is Christmas. It is such a busy time for most people, and our family is no exception. When I entered church for the Christmas Eve service, my mind was focused on tomorrow. What food still needed prepared? Did I forget to buy any gifts? Where do we need to be, and at what time on Christmas day? My head was pounding with a headache, mostly from the tension which I had brought upon myself. In the midst of the day's flurry, I had totally forgotten why we were celebrating Christmas. During the past few days, I'm not sure I had even taken the time to pray. Instead, I was worrying about all the preparations, and how there weren't enough hours in my day!

As we sang the traditional Christmas hymns, I began to relax. They were joyful, and the atmosphere was quiet. My mind slowly returned to the true meaning of Christmas as we worshiped, and the pastor gave the message. At the end of the service we were all holding lit candles. As I stood there holding my candle, my eyes were drawn to the flame. As I studied the flame, I could see two definite outlines and colors. The inner part, closer to the wick was darker and the outer part totally surrounded it and glowed. I focused on how my attitude changed during the service. As I became relaxed, and allowed the Holy Spirit to fill me, I began to glow. It was as if the Holy Spirit had surrounded me just as the glow surrounds the inner flame. It made me more beautiful, and allowed me to sway slightly to "O Holy Night," just as a flame sways in the breeze. The flame on the candle is radiant because of the outer glow. As Christians we too need to have an outer glow, and move gracefully.

Below in *Matthew 12:18–21* we read about the prophesy of *Isaiah 42* being fulfilled. Many people expected Christ to be a great ruler wearing a crown. Christ was a great Ruler, but in a different way. He ruled by allowing the Holy Spirit to come upon Him. Read these verses, and see how Jesus sets an example for you and me when we are filled with the Holy Spirit.

> *"Look at my Servant, whom I have chosen.*
> *He is my Beloved, who pleases me.*
> *I will put my Spirit upon him,*
> *and he will proclaim justice to the nations.*
> *He will not fight or shout*
> *or raise his voice in public.*
> *He will not crush the weakest reed*
> *or put out a flickering candle.*
> *Finally he will cause justice to be victorious.*
> *And his name will be the hope*
> *of all the world."*

"Hope of all the world." These are words to help you relax. No matter what is on your mind today, there is hope. So take some time to allow the Holy Spirit to fill you. May you resemble a candle, and have an outer glow as you face your day with a gentle spirit. May you sway in the breeze of life as you spread the news that Christ is the Hope of all the world.

STREAKED WINDOWS

Window washing it is not a household chore I love. As a matter of fact, I have to talk myself into accomplishing the job. It is a task which I only tackle once or twice a year, even though I should wash the windows more often. But on the flip side, once I clean the first window and see the results, I am determined to clean every window in the house, both inside and out. I am on a mission to have perfectly clean windows. Why, because they look so wonderful when the job is completed. Or do they?

There have been many times when I sat down at the end of a window washing day and just smiled. Life on the outside never looked so beautiful. No spots, no dust, no cobwebs just the bright setting sun shining through the clean sparkling windows. I sit back and enjoy the moment. Even though my arms ache from all the washing, and my legs and knees hurt from climbing up and down the ladder all day, I feel a sense of accomplishment. After a good night's sleep, I arise, look out the window and what do I see? STREAKS! I'm horrified! How can this be? They weren't streaked yesterday and since my body still has some aches and pains from the day before, I let out a big sigh. I am in no mood or condition to start over again today. I tell myself it is ok if they aren't perfect. If company should drop in, they will at least know that I tried to clean my windows.

Windows are so much like our Christian lives. When we accept Christ as our Savior, He washes our sins away and gives us a clean window to life. Life changes for us that very moment. We begin to see life through clean windows with no spots, or dust, or cobwebs. We are eager to complete every Christian task to the best of our ability. But we are by no means perfect, and it isn't long until we start to see the streaks in our own lives. The Son might be shining in the windows of our hearts, but unless we allow Him to continually wash away our dirt and clean our streaks, we lose focus in our Christian walk.

But there is great news. Just as a good friend would not see the streaks on our house windows, God doesn't see the streaks in our lives. *1 John 1:9 (NIV)* says, *"If we confess our sins, he is faithful and just and will forgive us our sins and purify us from all unrighteousness."* God is in the window washing business, called forgiveness. There is no need for us to worry about the streaks in our lives. Our job is to simply confess our sins and ask Him to clean the windows of our heart. He will grab His window cleaner and wipe away our sins. The good news is that tomorrow morning when you arise and the morning Son shines in, there will be no streaks. God keeps no record of our sins either. *Psalms 130:3–4 (MSG)* says, *"If you, God, kept records on wrongdoings, who would stand a chance? As it turns out, forgiveness is your habit, and that's why you're worshiped."*

Today, tomorrow, and every day here forward, ask God to clean the streaks off of the windows of your heart. Don't wait to wash the windows of your heart once or twice a year like I do the windows of my house. Daily confession of sin is so cleansing and refreshing. Always remember, He keeps no record of the streaks in your life. You start with a clean window each and every day. So let the Son shine in!

$\mathcal{B}$OBSLED RIDE

My husband, Jim, and I are ready for a new adventure whenever we get the chance. One particular trip, we traveled with our friends. The decision was made to drive from Lake Tahoe, down through the snow covered, winding mountains, through Yosemite with a final destination of King's Canyon to see the giant sequoia trees.

A new adventure it was as we left Lake Tahoe! Since we are used to Ohio winters, we didn't realize that in early March, there would still be a wall of snow on both sides of the road as we came down the mountains. A side bit of info here, the license plate on my car says, I LOVE JR, with JR being my hubby's initials. I am often asked if I love Dale Earnhardt, Jr. Well, this was one time where Jim instantly turned into Dale Earnhardt, Jr. Off he drove or should I say flew! Have you ever seen those four men bobsleds on the Olympics? Well I think he secretly entered us in the competition!

We swerved, turned, and flew around corners. Fortunately, he is a good driver and we never bounced off the snow walls coming down the mountain. We were also winning, because no other vehicles ever passed us! We were tossed around in the back seat of the SUV like a couple of marbles in a jar. Plus the farther he drove, the faster he seemed to go!

As if the adventure wasn't exciting enough, or should I say scary enough, I'm prone to car sickness in the back seat of some vehicles. Of course this SUV happened to be one of them. I vaguely remember the first stop flying by, as I muttered from the back seat.

"Honey, I don't feel well. Could you stop?" I'm not sure if it was selective hearing, because he was having fun or if he truly did not hear me moaning from the back seat.

Regardless, when the next available stop approached, I loudly proclaimed from the back seat, "If you don't stop, I'm going to puke on your head!" Now that got his attention and he promptly pulled over.

We crawled out of the back seat. My friend seriously considered kissing the ground, as she was still alive. Our other friend who was in the passenger seat unlocked his knuckles from what my son refers to as the "Oh help me Jesus handle." (Obviously our son has ridden with Jim in the mountains before.) Jim gets out, stretches and says, "Isn't this fun. Look at all this snow." To which one of us replied, "Is that what that white stuff is flying by?"

It was at this point Jim noticed we all looked slightly green, and muttered, "I was just having a little fun. We can't fall off the mountain. There is snow on both sides to keep us on the road."

Do you ever feel as if your life is a bobsled ride? Twists, turns, walls on both sides, and you just try to go down the middle without bouncing over the edge. Well I have good news! God is leading us through this slalom called life. We just need to let Him drive our bobsled.

I guarantee the journey you are on will be worth the ride, no matter how many twists and turns you take. Jim did slow down so we could enjoy the scenery and I got over my car sickness. Oh, what beautiful sights God has created for our pleasure.

God creates beautiful scenery in our lives every day! He has been teaching me to slow down my bobsled this past year. *Psalm 46:10* says, *"Be still, and know that I am God!"* When I slow down, I tend to see the brighter side of life. I enjoy the simple things like occasionally babysitting for my niece, and enjoying their kids. I take time to notice beautiful sunsets, or stars twinkling in the evening sky. God intends for us to not only enjoy the beauty of life, but the curves and bumps in the road as well. When we hit the twists and turns in life, it is important to be still and listen to the One who is the Captain of your bobsled because He will lead you safely down the mountain.

FALL HARVEST

Fall harvest on the farm can be stressful at times. The days are long, the weather can be cold, and the sun sets early. It is a constant battle to achieve as much as possible each day, usually because the next rain is on the way. Often tempers can flare due to the lack of patience, and it can be heard in our voices.

This particular harvest was no different. While working in the dark unloading grain, some of it spilled onto the ground. Being a fairly new wife on the farm and not used to the fast pace, I felt very hurt and dejected when my husband left me behind in the dark to clean up the mess while he returned to the field for another load of corn. His reason was that it had to be completed because rain was coming during the night. Maybe it was the tone of his voice or his lack of patience that upset me. I'm not sure. I completed the task the best way I knew how. Not with a helpful heart but with tears of frustration running down my cheeks. The entire time thinking to myself, "I didn't sign up for this! Why do I have to clean up this mess?"

Because I was upset, I sat on the back porch of my in-laws home awaiting my husband's return, rather than going in where it was warm. I just felt the need to sit and sulk in my own misery, sort of having a self pity party. After quite some time my mother-in-law, Leah, found me on the porch, cold, shivering and crying. She insisted that I come in and have a cup of coffee. Now she knew I didn't drink coffee, but it was her way of saying, "Let's sit and talk."

The first words she said were, "We just need to pray for patience and strength this time of year."

Leah always had a way of speaking such calming words and they were always words with such wisdom. As I look back on that day, I wonder how many times I have told God, "I didn't sign up for this!" God often asks us to do what is impossible by our standards, but *Philippians 4:13* says, *"For I can do everything through Christ, who gives me strength."* Sometimes the trials in our lives are God's way of strengthening us for His future work. Only He knows what our future holds.

I also wonder how many opportunities I have missed during my life because I didn't take the time to have a cup of coffee with God. The old hymn, "What A Friend We Have In Jesus,'" says...

> "O what peace we often forfeit,
> O what needless pain we bear,
> All because we do not carry,
> Everything to God in prayer!"

So when life's frustrations get you down, don't sit outside on the porch in the cold. Come into His warm loving arms, quote *Philippians 4:13* and have a cup of coffee with God. You will be amazed at the outcome!

Points to Ponder

- How often does your voice reflect impatience, rather than encouragement and helpfulness?
- How many times have you felt life wasn't fair and didn't complete a task or did so reluctantly?
- During those times, did you ask God to give you strength and patience for the trial in your life?
- Have you taken time to have a cup of coffee with God today? Remember to carry everything to God in prayer.

$\mathcal{C}$ountry Road

I live in the country on your typical back road. It is complete with curves, potholes, narrow tunnel areas and wildlife. I'm sure you have traveled such a road during your lifetime.

Most mornings, because I'm so accustomed to the drive, I fly down the road, and around the curves—assuming no one is coming. It is like my daily walk with Christ, sometimes I get too accustomed to the routine. I might say "Good morning God," a quick thank you, and I'm on my way for the day. But sometimes this way of life can be dangerous, because you don't know what is around the curve.

The truth is God doesn't promise life will always be easy. He actually says it will be hard. Christ speaks of this in *John 16:33b (NIV)*. *"In this world you will have trouble. But take heart! I have overcome the world."* Occasionally you have to slow down on the curves of life and ask God for guidance.

Many summers our road becomes a tunnel with trees on one side and tall corn on the other. You cannot see oncoming traffic around the curves. You have to proceed slowly having faith no one will be coming quickly toward you. Sometimes God expects this same action from us in life. *Hebrews 11:1 (NIV)* says, *"Now faith is being sure of what we hope for and certain of what we do not see."* God wants us to walk by faith and not by sight. Having faith that He will lead us through this tunnel called life.

And of course, there are the potholes. When you hit one, it jars the car and you think, "Why didn't I see it coming!" Life sometimes hits us with hardships when we least expect. Maybe your son is failing in school or your daughter has an eating disorder. You stop and wonder, "Why didn't I see that coming!"

Occasionally there are obstacles in the road such as wildlife. You have to slam on the brakes to prevent hitting the animal. Maybe you had to slam on the brakes due to an illness, death in the family, divorce, or loss of a job. You instantly stop, attempting to recover from the shock of some upsetting news.

There is a unique part to my morning drive to work. Lately most mornings the neighbor's horse greets me as I round the first corner. As if he is saying, "Good morning, I'm here." He is there to guide me around the second corner and see me safely to the stop sign at the end of the road. Christ wants to be our guide in life as well. When we take time to look around we see His guiding hand in everything we do. He is there to lead us around the curves and shine a light into our tunnel of life! God promises this in *Proverbs 4:1, "I will teach you wisdom's ways and lead you in straight paths."*

So the next time you hit a pothole, go around a curve, through a tunnel, or stop dead in your tracks, don't forget to talk to Christ, for He will lead you and keep you safe.

Points to Ponder

- Are there any potholes in your road of life which you have been driving around? Talk to God about them instead.
- Spend a few extra moments praying for the loved ones in your life who need extra care.

Our curvy, country road

CIRCLE OF FAITH

Faith is an element in my life, which I have questioned from time to time. What exactly is faith? *Hebrews 11:1 (NIV)* tells us that "*Faith is confidence in what we hope for and assurance about what we do not see.*" But what if I pray for something in faith and it doesn't happen? Is that lack of faith? I have come to realize over the years that it is not. Sometimes, God just says "No," and I'm thankful that He does.

I had the good fortune of growing up in a godly home, where examples of faith surrounded me daily. Since I grew up on a family farm, there was a great deal of work, but there were also many lessons of faith each and every day. I watched year after year as my father had faith that the seeds he planted would grow. They needed to receive the right amount of rain, sunshine and nutrients to produce a crop to provide for his dairy cattle and an income to support his family.

I observed my mother, who was definitely a *Proverbs 31* woman. She had the faith necessary to stretch my dad's income to provide for their five children. Her faith showed her how to be a farm wife, gardener, seamstress, nurse, cook, and mother. She had faith in herself and God as she faced the challenges of being a young wife and mother. Faith God would give her strength for each new day and help her provide for the needs of her family.

As a very little girl, I remember my Grandpa Robinson quoting scripture to his grandchildren. I didn't realize it then, but he was teaching me the importance of knowing God's Word at a very young age.

I am blessed with fond memories of my Grandma Conklin, who invested in my life. She not only spoiled me like any grandma should, she showed me what it was like to be active in her church. As a widow, she held firm to her beliefs. She invested herself in the lives of others by teaching Sunday school, preparing dinners at the church, and many other activities with the ladies. Regardless of the day's activities, she always saved the end of the day for Jesus. Every evening was saved for prayer and reading her Bible. As a young child, I was observing her, and logging all of this information for future reference. She was molding me, and left a huge imprint on my heart as I learned from her examples.

Growing up I attended Sunday school and church every Sunday. I knew the Bible stories like all the other children at church. It just didn't take root in my heart as a tangible part of my life. In spite of all this wonderful upbringing, I had to find faith in God on my own. It wasn't until I came to the end of myself, that I found a lifeline to sustain me in the days to come. Christ became my hope and my future.

Following a divorce and being a single mother of two, I found myself looking back to my roots. It seemed that my bad choices in life had piled one on top of another, until the only place left to look was up. I sat upon my sofa one lonely evening and cried out to God. I found myself wrapped in His loving arms as I asked Him to give my life new purpose and direction. It was a private time between God and me as I rededicated my life to Him that tearful night. The following morning, I rose with a new confidence in myself, and the situation because it was now in Christ's hands. I knew from experience and the examples God had given me in my roots that He would not let me down. I knew the path ahead may be rocky, but it would be the right one because God was leading for the first time in my adult life.

Unknown to me, following his divorce, my husband Jim was praying for a companion in his life as well. God heard our prayers and set us on a path to meet one another. The rest is history, as we have now been married for twenty-five years. He is the love of my life, and he took me back to my roots—the farm. Of course there have been rough days, squabbles, and a lot of hard work on the farm. In spite of any problems we encounter, we never lose focus on the fact that God brought two lonely, messed up lives together. He took what we called a mess, and made it something beautiful.

I was blessed with more Christian roots as well. I was given a mother-in-law who taught me more lessons in faith. No matter the circumstances, problem, or decision we faced on the farm, it was so simple to Leah. She would simply say, "We just need to have faith and pray." Her faith in God was shown as she walked daily with the Lord, and prayed for her family and friends. She went home to be with the Lord many years ago. Seldom does a day go by where I don't think of her, and the godly woman she was. Jim often says he misses the daily prayers he knows his mother was sending up on his behalf.

My faith has taken me full circle in life, as our sons grew up on the farm just as I was raised. They are both in the agriculture business, and also working on the family farm. Jim and I have tried to instill in their lives the importance of having faith in God from the smallest decision, to the biggest one. I thank God that He took my messed up life, and set my feet on the right path. As a result, my children were surrounded with the same foundation and roots which I had the privilege of knowing.

As life goes full circle, I look forward to being a mentor of faith to my daughters-in-law, as both sons are married now. I pray that one day my grandchildren will see me saving the end of every day for Jesus, or hear me quote a Bible verse. I'm hoping to plant a seed of faith in their hearts in the future. I pray that I have successfully planted the seeds of faith in my sons. One lonely evening, they too may journey to the sofa, and Christ will become a more tangible piece of their lives. My hope is that the circle of faith will continue for many generations to come as they hear Leah's familiar words through me, "We just need to have faith and pray."

$\mathcal{D}$UCKS IN THE FIELD

It is late June and the rain hasn't stopped for weeks. The weeds are taking over some fields because we can't even spray. One field has been replanted, and still may not have a crop. While driving by one of our fields on my way to church, I noticed that one entire corner was so flooded that the only thing growing were mallard ducks! I mentioned to my son, "We are growing ducks on Hoskins Road! How much are they worth?" In his usual sense of humor he replied, "Well at least we will have meat to eat, but they taste a little gamey." We didn't eat the ducks, but his witty humor lightened my mood about the flood in our field.

Farming is a true test of faith. Like this year, farmers may have too much rain and can't get into the fields to work. On other years, drought may be a problem. When farmers experience weather problems, it makes us appreciate the years when weather is so perfect. There is no doubt that tension runs high, and the worries pile up when the weather isn't favorable. Why do we allow ourselves to react this way? Farmers can't control the weather, all they can do is make the best decisions possible under the circumstances. We can pray desperate prayers (and believe me we have) asking God to turn off the rain or send the rain. Does He here our prayers? Absolutely! Sometimes it just isn't the answer we would like.

When we walk through difficult times like these, we tend to hear common phrases such as: It is in the valleys of life that you grow.

God never gives you more than you can handle. A day hemmed in prayer seldom comes unraveled.

I believe all of these statements are true, but when times are difficult, these cliché statements provide little comfort. True comfort comes from our faith in God and reading His Word. Backing these statements up with biblical truths makes them more comforting.

Psalm 34:17–19 (NIV) tells us that when we are in the valleys of life, we need to seek the Lord and He will help us grow. *"The righteous cry out, and the L*ORD* hears them; he delivers them from all their troubles. The L*ORD* is close to the brokenhearted and saves those who are crushed in spirit. The righteous person may have many troubles, but the L*ORD* delivers him from them all."*

As it says in *2 Corinthians 12:10 (NIV)*, God never gives us more than we can handle, because He is our source of strength *"That is why, for Christ's sake, I delight in weaknesses, in insults, in hardships, in persecutions, in difficulties. For when I am weak, then I am strong."* Our strength and contentment need to come from the Lord. *"I have learned to be content whatever the circumstances... I have learned the secret of being content in any and every situation... I can do all this through him who gives me strength"* Philippians 4:11–13 (NIV).

Luke 5:16 tells us that when Jesus felt like His day was coming unraveled, He spent time in prayer seeking the Father's will. *"But Jesus often withdrew to the wilderness for prayer."* We need to follow Christ's example and spend quiet time with God. It is during these quiet moments that we can cry out to Him for strength through the difficulties of life.

God placed the mallard ducks in the field that day to get my attention. Yes we have had too much rain. But God provided manna for the Israelites, and He will provide for us. God created everything including the birds of the air. So He sent me two beautiful mallard ducks to brighten my spirits on a dreary day. I need to do my part and change my attitude. Rather than focusing on the poor farming conditions, I need to apply biblical truths to my life, and praise Him for all of my blessings. He is my Deliverer, my Strength, and my Solace.

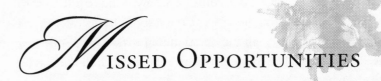

MISSED OPPORTUNITIES

Then Naomi heard in Moab that the LORD had blessed his people in Judah by giving them good crops again. So Naomi and her daughters-in-law got ready to leave Moab to return to her homeland. With her two daughters-in-law she set out from the place where she had been living, and they took the road that would lead them back to Judah. But on the way, Naomi said to her two daughters-in-law, "Go back to your mothers' homes. And may the LORD reward you for your kindness to your husbands and to me. May the LORD bless you with the security of another marriage." Then she kissed them good-bye, and they all broke down and wept....And again they wept together, and Orpah kissed her mother-in-law good-bye. But Ruth clung tightly to Naomi. "Look," Naomi said to her, "your sister-in-law has gone back to her people and to her gods. You should do the same." (Ruth 1:6–9, 14–15)

As the book of Ruth continues there are wonderful lessons to learn as Ruth and Naomi return to Judah. But when I read the beginning of this story, I always have questions about Orpah. The story tells us that Orpah returned to Moab, and nothing more. We are left wondering—Did she make it to Moab safely? Did she return to her gods, or did she continue to worship Naomi's God in a pagan land? Was Orpah too scared to leave Moab, and jumped at the chance to stay? The questions continue in my mind. But I have to accept the fact that God didn't write the rest of Orpah's story for a reason. There is one remaining question that makes me ponder my own life. Did Orpah miss an opportunity to serve God, and have a different life?

I missed an opportunity to minister to a friend once. Her mother had recently become very ill and passed away a very short time later. I was so consumed by my own career problems that I wasn't there for my friend. Every word I said, and every action I showed did not reflect my love for her and her mother. I didn't begin to express the pain I felt for them during their time of loss. Oh, what a missed opportunity to be the hands and feet of Christ. As time healed my broken heart from the pain I caused my friend I wondered, "How many other people did I hurt along the way during that tumultuous time of my life?"

In our lives, there will be times when we miss opportunities. A chance to advance in your career. An opportunity for love. Precious moments to serve Christ. The prospect of starting a new life. Just to name a few. The important thing to remember is that God never lets us miss an opportunity without stretching us and teaching us. *Proverbs 16:9* tells us *"We can make our plans, but the LORD determines our steps."* Maybe that missed opportunity in my life was really part of God's plan to help me grow into a better Christian. Or could it be that the missed opportunity in your life is because you were too afraid to leave "Moab" and step out in faith. If so God is the God of second chances. When you think you have totally blown it, God can turn that moment around into something beautiful as you learn from your mistakes. God blesses us with His grace and gives us many chances to follow Him. He turns every missed opportunity into a teaching moment and allows us to change the outcome of our future.

Ruth chose to continue on with Naomi to Judah and to serve Naomi's God. God rewarded her for that choice. Boaz married Ruth and she became part of the lineage of Jesus Christ! Orpah chose to return to Moab. Did God reward Orpah too or did she face difficult times when she returned to Moab? Naomi prayed that Orpah would be blessed with the security of another marriage. I like to believe that God heard Naomi's request and blessed her as well. Orpah and Ruth definitely made different choices in their lives. Just simply reading the book of Ruth tells us that God will reward those who follow Him. Regardless of our mistakes, God will bless us for returning and being faithful.

Unlike Orpah's story, you can write the end of your story and others will know the outcome. Don't allow the fear of the unknown keep you from serving an amazing God. And don't be like me and allow a messed up career stop you from being a friend at a crucial time in your life. Step forward and allow the Holy Spirit to guide you wherever He is calling you today as He rewrites the next chapter of your life.

AULA

Paula is such a familiar name in our household. Unfortunately, the reason her name is so familiar is the constant prayers going up on her behalf for the past several years. I was praying for her before I ever met her. A mutual friend had told us about her battle with cancer and asked that we add her name to our prayer list. God in his sovereignty knew that we would one day meet in person as we now attend the same church.

Paula has faced this courageous battle of stage four breast cancer in a quiet, God is with me attitude. Every day is new each morning to her *(Lamentations 3:22–24)*, and the Lord is her strength *(Nehemiah 8:10)*. She never loses hope of God's will as she travels this journey. Not only has she amazed her doctors by far exceeding their expectations, she is an example of the power of prayer. While her personality is to live a quiet life with her circle of friends by her side, her husband Jeff shares her stories, and battles with others. Just by being God's silent servant, the number of lives she has touched is amazing. God asks us to be a witness and in Paula's case that witness is to face each day knowing God is in control. Whenever the doctors give her bad news, she just calls it another bump in the road. What an example of faith in such a simple statement.

God has blessed her with many more days here on earth with her family than were ever thought possible at the onset. Along her path, Paula has met nurses who prayed the scriptures over her and sang beautiful hymns. There was a patient awaiting an MRI herself who prayed for her. She witnessed Paula in pain going in for an MRI and Jeff with his Bible in hand. She quickly realized her illness wasn't as severe as Paula's and started to pray. God's blessings continue to flow down upon the family as they live each moment for Christ.

When life gets me down, it is so easy to have a pity party. But as I witness this remarkable woman of faith, I realize my problems are nothing. As I sit on the sidelines praying for Paula, God has stretched my faith by watching her endure this battle without wavering. From Paula, I have learned that every prayer is important as I have witnessed the power of prayer on her behalf. I don't have to be in the inner circle to be a part of the solution. God calls us to pray continuously. How many times have I passed up an opportunity to pray for someone because I didn't really know them? After all *Colossians 4:2 (NIV)* says, *"Devote yourselves to prayer, being watchful and thankful."*

Paula's journey is a wonderful example of a person who follows *Philippians 4:5–7 (NIV)*.

> *Let your gentleness be evident to all. The Lord is near.*
> *Do not be anxious about anything, but in everything,*
> *by prayer and petition, with thanksgiving, present*
> *your requests to God. And the peace of God, which*
> *transcends all understanding, will guard your hearts*
> *and your minds in Christ Jesus.*

May God's blessings continue to flow down upon Paula as she lives a life exemplary of this passage of scripture! And may each of us continue to learn about the power of prayer from the sidelines of her life.

Paula finished her walk here on this earth and is now rejoicing in heaven with her Savior. Her family and friends did not tell her goodbye, they simply told her that they would see her later. What a testimony of their faith! I will forever be grateful for the many lessons I learned from this wonderful lady. Her humor, compassion for her family, love for God, endurance and perseverance has forever impacted my life, and the lives of all who knew her.

 NAMES OF GOD

Sometimes in our Christian walks we are so busy doing ministry that we lose our focus on who God is. We complete the next Bible study and read all the books. We serve on committees and plan events. We do mission work and tithe. We counsel and witness. But we spend very little time with God. The busyness of ministry isn't always worship and focusing on the love of God. Today take a few moments to contemplate on the names of God and their meanings in your life.

Billy Sunday once said, "There are two hundred and fifty-six names given in the Bible for the Lord Jesus Christ, and I suppose this was because He was infinitely beyond all that any one name could express." Spend time in prayer and meditation as you focus on the Author of your soul and all He has to offer.

God replied to Moses, "I AM WHO I AM. Say this to
the people of Israel: I AM has sent me to you."
Exodus 3:14

And he will be called: Wonderful Counselor, Mighty
God, Everlasting Father, Prince of Peace.
Isaiah 9:6b

"I am the good shepherd. The good shepherd
sacrifices his life for the sheep."
John 10:11

"These are the words of the Amen, the faithful and
true witness, the ruler of God's creation."
Revelation 3:14b (NIV)

Comforter

Almighty

Carpenter ~ **Most High**

Adonai ~ **Ancient of Days**

Elohim ~ Love ~ Yahweh ~ God

Firstborn ~ Everlasting Father

Anointed One ~ Prince of Peace ~ *Door* ~ Teacher ~ Lamb of God

Counselor ~ **CHRIST** ~ *Physician* ~ **Consuming** *Fire* ~ Mediator

Protector ~ End ~ Lord of Lords ~ Keeper ~ **Guide** ~ Helper ~ All in All

Redeemer ~ **Alpha** ~ *Jehovah* ~ SHEPHERD ~ *Omega* ~ King of Kings ~ **Life**

El-Shaddai ~ Bridegroom ~ Word ~ Friend ~ *Prince of Life* ~ Bright Morning Star

Breath of Life ~ **Jesus** ~ *King of Glory* ~ **Mighty God** ~ Savior

Master ~ Maker ~ *The Vine* ~ Portion ~ *Creator* ~ The Way

Cornerstone ~ *Deliverer* ~ Emmanuel ~ Fortress ~ Leader

BREAD OF LIFE ~ *Commander* ~ Abba ~ **Rock**

Potter ~ **Wonderful** ~ Branch

I Am ~ Highest ~ *Truth*

Living Water ~ Hope

THE LIGHT

Amen

Points to Ponder

- At this current moment in time, which name describes your relationship with God?
- In the past when you needed God most, how would you describe Him?
- We don't know what our future holds, so which definition of God will you need?

$\mathcal{S}$EQUOIA TREES

My husband and I love to travel and see some of the beautiful scenery which God has created for all of us to enjoy. One year during our winter vacation we traveled through Yosemite National Park where we saw a cascading waterfall with snow capped mountains. What a symbol of God's love flowing down upon us. But our final destination was King's Canyon to see the giant sequoia forest. Enormous trees which reach up toward heaven. The branches were covered in white fluffy snow, with huge snow drifts all around. The park was so quiet and peaceful.

We walked around, totally amazed and I said, "The only thing that could make this more beautiful is if it were snowing right now." Wouldn't you know it, God heard me! Within a few minutes a dark cloud moved in, and huge snowflakes began to fall to the ground. God blessed me with His presence and the beautiful trees that day.

We can become just like giant sequoia trees with God's help. Did you know that giant sequoia trees actually thrive in forest fires? Their thick bark protects them from the flames. The fire thins the forest of pines and firs, which would normally overtake young sequoia trees. Also the sequoia trees shed the most seeds following a fire. These seeds grow best in fire mineralized soil, so new growth is started as a result of the fire.

This is so much like you and me. God will test us in the flames of life, but He also provides us with His protection of love and grace. Once we have been through the fire, He will take our hurts and pain, and fertilize them with love. We will spring up with new growth, compassion and understanding. The fires of life are just preparing us to become a more affective part of the body of Christ.

When we take the burned pieces of our lives and give them to God, He will turn them into something beautiful. How has God turned the burnt pieces of your life into something beautiful? For me, He has turned the divorce in my life into a witnessing tool to help others. The financially lean years of being a single mom, taught me the importance of giving to those in need. The family trials I have faced in the last few years, have taught me to lend a listening ear to friends. All of my experiences help me to become an active member of the body of Christ, reaching out and ministering to those in need.

> *I look up to the mountains; does my strength come from mountains? No, my strength comes from God, who made heaven, and earth, and mountains. He won't let you stumble; your Guardian God won't fall asleep. Not on your life! Israel's Guardian will never doze or sleep. (Psalm 121:1–3 MSG)*

I pray you will allow God to help you grow into a strong and beautiful giant sequoia tree, so He can use you to share His love with others. May you find your gifts and passions as God leads you through the fires of life. May you hear God walking through the forest of life and follow Him wherever He leads you in ministry.

So I Might Serve

You hung upon the tree.
The pain you bore for me.
My sins You take away.
Heart of love You portray.

Sacrificial blood of Lamb.
You are the great I Am.
You came to set me free.
My heart you hold the key.

You rose again to be,
My King, oh yes indeed.
You know my hurt and pain.
You help me to sustain.

From You all blessings flow.
With you O Lord, I grow.
Please use me as I am.
A servant of the Lamb.

Spirit from high above.
Please fill my heart with love.
Lord, open wide the doors,
So I might serve You more.

ULTIMATE GIFT

We recently celebrated Christmas and we had a wonderful evening with our family. Reflecting back on the night, there was one exciting moment when my husband, Jim, opened his big package. Our son Matt could not wait for Jim to open the package because he knew that he had given him the ultimate Christmas present in that big box. Typically we go around the room taking turns. If you have fewer packages, you can pass until the next round to space out your unveiling. Well my husband had the least number of packages, so he continually passed. After a couple of rounds of this, Matt insisted that Jim start opening presents. Well of course he didn't open the big one. He was saving it for last. We continued to go around and Jim continued to pass. Finally Matt couldn't stand it anymore and said, "Open the big box!" As soon as Jim slid the box close, Matt was on his feet to see his expression as he opened the gift.

Inside the package was a framed poster which contained pictures of the farm. Matt had been shooting and accumulating pictures for over two years. He had sorted out some of the best pictures and had them made into a poster. The pictures included: various pieces of equipment working in the field, construction on the grain system and our different farms. Matt had taken a great deal of time to come up with the perfect Christmas gift. He used his time and talent to take beautiful, unique pictures of the farm which he presented in the form of a gift with great enthusiasm. Jim was in total awe of the poster. It was like a dream come true for him to have a picture of the farm showing a small part of his journey. He grew up on the farm and had taken over the operation from his father, and now our sons, Matt and Ryan, are part of the farm. At that moment in time it was the ultimate gift as we all stopped opening packages to look at each picture on the poster.

For those of us who are Christians, we also have tucked away in our hearts the knowledge of the Ultimate Gift. That gift is the birth of Christ. *"She gave birth to her first child, a son. She wrapped him snugly in strips of cloth and laid him in a manger, because there was no lodging available for them"* (Luke 2:7).

His miraculous birth was followed by His death on the cross. *"Then Jesus shouted, 'Father, I entrust my spirit into your hands!' And with those words he breathed his last"* (Luke 34:46).

And ultimately His amazing resurrection from the grave!

> *The women were terrified and bowed with their faces to the ground. Then the men asked, "Why are you looking among the dead for someone who is alive? He isn't here! He is risen from the dead! Remember what he told you back in Galilee, that the Son of Man must be betrayed into the hands of sinful men and be crucified, and that he would rise again on the third day." (Luke 24:5–7)*

Do we give away the knowledge of our Ultimate Gift and the fact that He brings us eternal life, with the same enthusiasm Matt presented his ultimate Christmas gift? Sometimes we hold tightly to the gift as if it is only for us. The gift Matt presented was as much a part of his life as it is Jim's life which added to his excitement. At times we don't allow ourselves to get involved because it requires us to give of ourselves and to connect with others. When we truly accept Christ as a part of our daily lives, sharing the Gift, and serving others becomes natural. We begin to share and serve with enthusiasm and joy. Matt used talent and time to create an ultimate

Christmas gift, a gift which came from the heart. Is Christ such a deep part of your life that you want to use your talent and time to spread the knowledge of His love to others?

We have all been called to share the blessing of the Ultimate Gift with others. I pray you find a way to reach out to others and share the message of your Ultimate Gift, Jesus Christ.

> *Then Jesus came to them and said, "All authority in heaven and on earth has been given to me. Therefore go and make disciples of all nations, baptizing them in the name of the Father and of the Son and of the Holy Spirit, and teaching them to obey everything I have commanded you. And surely I am with you always, to the very end of the age." (Matthew 28:18–20)*

SPIRITUAL BLINDNESS

I awoke a couple of nights ago taking short, quick breaths. I'm not sure it qualifies as a nightmare, but it was definitely a dream which I don't care to repeat in my real life. It was very vivid with color, noise, and confusion all rolled into one. Of course I laid awake for a couple of minutes catching my breath and wondered what the dream meant.

In my dream I was driving and about to merge onto a very busy freeway. Just as the two lanes were merging into one, I was suddenly blinded. Every time I tried to open my eyes to see traffic, there was a bright light. It was so brilliant it reminded me of being snow blind, and I was forced to close my eyes again. I could hear horns honking and semi trucks barreling by me. I would struggle to open my eyes, but I just couldn't see! I eventually pulled the car to the right and could tell by the change in the pavement that I was on the shoulder of the road and came to a stop. As I struggled to see, I was able to see quick glimpses of traffic flying by me. Whew, thank goodness I was safe! You can imagine how thankful I was to open my eyes and find myself lying in bed! It is very unusual for me to remember my dreams, but this one was still vivid at daybreak and I shared it with my husband.

How many times in our lives are we spiritually blind? Just as I was blind in my dream, we can be blind in our walk with Christ. Spiritual blindness can be just as scary, but the good news is that we don't have to walk through life spiritually blind.

Knowing God is more than just believing that He exists. Knowing God is having a relationship with Him. Let's look at an example of a good friend. You are friends because you have a relationship together. You talk to one another, you listen to one another. You help and care for each other. My dream is significant simply because it is an example of how you can feel walking through life spiritually blind. If you don't have a relationship with Christ, which models a relationship with your friend, you don't really know Him. You won't be able to see Christ in your life. You can't call him Friend, or Pilot without that personal relationship.

When I have a bond with Jesus, I talk to Him and listen to Him. When problems come my way, I need to ask for strength, discernment and direction. Seeing hope in Jesus during difficulties helps me to build a stronger relationship. There are days I might pray, "Your will be done today Lord." Yet at the end of day, I wonder if all my difficulties are truly His will. When the day doesn't go as planned, I need to ask Jesus what lessons I am to learn from my complicated day.

> *I keep asking that the God of our Lord Jesus Christ,
> the glorious Father, may give you the Spirit of wisdom
> and revelation, so that you may know him better. I
> pray that the eyes of your heart may be enlightened
> in order that you may know the hope to which he has
> called you, the riches of his glorious inheritance in his
> holy people, and his incomparably great power for us
> who believe. (Ephesians 1:17–19a NIV)*

There is a popular praise song titled, "Open the Eyes of My Heart" written by Paul Baloche. Maybe today you should ask God to open your spiritual eyes that you might see Him more clearly. Don't be blinded by the bright light and the honking of horns as life passes you by on the freeway of life. Tell Jesus you want to see Him in everything, both the good and the bad. As He opens the eyes of your heart, you will find yourself calling Him Friend.

FAMILY LEGACY

A good life gets passed on to the grandchildren.
Proverbs 13:22a (MSG)

Today I was sorting some of my sister's Bible study books to donate. At a quick glance through some papers I found a note which spoke volumes about our Christian heritage. The question in the book said, "Have you ever heard a great Christian testimony and wished you could have the faith of that person or live as he or she has lived?" Linda's reply was, "My grandmother. She read and prayed all of her life." I was so surprised to see these words, but I should not have been. I have said the same words about Grandma all my life. I suddenly realized that this was the model for her life, a part of her legacy for her grandchildren. From the oldest grandchild to the youngest, we observed the same actions.

A few years before Linda passed away, she attended the Walk to Emmaus. The weekend is a wonderful time to reflect on your life and grow closer to Christ. Ironically, the weekend dramatically changed Linda's prayer life. It was never the same following the weekend. She said she could feel God's presence when she prayed, and became a prayer warrior for others. Just like Grandma, her legacy included reading and praying.

I am so blessed to have come from a Christian background. I have always been surrounded with wonderful examples of faith in friends and family. As I grow older I realize that my focus needs to change from me to the generations to come. I need to remember that others are watching me. They are asking questions and looking to me for advice. It seems like only yesterday I was following in the footsteps of my parents and grandparents. Following their example and their advice. I don't want others to stumble, because I'm not setting a good Christian example. My growth as a Christian isn't just for me, but for the legacy I leave. What a huge responsibility to pass these great values on so others will know about Jesus. I pray that they come to understand that when you walk with Jesus and talk to Him continually, obstacles simply become a means of strengthening your faith.

My grandchildren are young, with the oldest being only four. But I want to live a life that reflects Jesus as they grow. Using small teachable moments such as dinner time prayers, or singing "Jesus Loves Me" will help build a foundation for greater faith as they grow. Little eyes are watching my every move and absorbing all of my actions, so my walk needs to reflect the love of Christ.

Leaving a Christian legacy is more than attending church on Sunday morning, and more than reading and praying like Grandma. It is about the life you live, when others are watching, and when they are not. How do you react during stressful times? Are you walking with Jesus daily through study, prayer and meditation? Are you treating others with respect? How are your work ethics? Are you a good witness for Christ? There are many questions you can ask yourself. The way we live our lives shows our devotion to the Lord.

Over the years I have learned more patience, and with that patience comes searching for God's wisdom in the Bible. That wisdom has made my faith stronger in the Lord. That strong faith has helped me through many difficult situations in my life. That faith has brought me to a stronger prayer life as I rely heavily on my relationship with the Lord.

For Grandma, reading her Bible and praying was the foundation of her Christian legacy. I pray my children and grandchildren see within me such a strong faith that they too will desire that personal walk with the Lord. I will have accomplished great works for Jesus if one day my grandchildren say, "Grandma, she read and prayed all of her life." Why? Because *a good life gets passed on to the grandchildren.*

PRICELESS MOMENT

One evening this week, Dad called to see if I was home. After telling him that I would be home, he replied, "Ok, we will see you in a little bit." My curiosity peaked, because it is very unusual for Mom and Dad to just pop in, especially at that time of the day. My first guess was that he needed my signature on some paperwork or there was something unusual to discuss. About fifteen minutes later Mom and Dad walked in the door. Dad was leading the way as they said, "Happy Mother's Day." There he was, shuffling along, a huge smile on his face, carrying a dozen red roses! I was so surprised. It was such a heartfelt moment. My father not only bought me roses, but he personally delivered them. It was just one of the priceless moments in my life. I mean truly priceless!

I have reflected on that special moment and the look on Dad's face all week. My friends have all heard me say, "I received a dozen red roses from Dad." I have been blessed to have a wonderful, loving father all of my life. It saddens me to think there are many who do not have that privilege. What a blessing from God that my earthly father is an example of the love my Heavenly Father shows me. Abba Father has those same feelings for each and every one of us. He cares for us more deeply than we can even fathom.

God cares about your comings and goings *(Psalm 121:8)*. During our Christian walks, God refines us like silver so that we grow *(Psalm 66:10)*. He forgives, heals and strengthens us. He shows us love and compassion *(Psalm 103)*. He keeps track of all your sorrows and saves your tears in a bottle *(Psalm 56:8)*. Every day of your life has been written in His book and planned out before you were born *(Psalm 139:16)*. You are so important to God that He has even numbered every hair on your head *(Matthew 10:29–31)*. Most importantly, you have been adopted by Christ into His own family *(Ephesians 1:5)*.

Don't let the priceless moments in life pass you by. It was a short visit the day I received my roses. They visited only a few minutes and then strolled back out the door. My Dad is eighty-nine years old and I cherish every moment I can spend with him. From the good times to the bad, the hard work and fun times, the tough conversations and the wisdom he has offered over the years. Each moment in its own special way has been priceless. Unfortunately, one day these precious moments will be nothing more than a memory as time marches on.

But for our Heavenly Father time doesn't change. He always was, always is, and always will be your Abba Father. Slow down from the busyness of life and cherish priceless moments with your Abba Father. They too will be unforgettable!

Suggested Scripture Reading

- *Ephesians 1:20*
- *Philippians 3:20*
- *Romans 8:1*
- *Romans 8:35*
- *John 1:12*

Beautiful red roses from Dad

CANDLES

It had been a very long, emotionally draining day for me. I was with my parents at the doctor's office when my mother received the sad news that she had pancreatic cancer. I had the task of telling my siblings, several nieces and nephews, my close friends, and my own family about Mom's diagnosis. With what seemed like only a few minutes of rest and silence to myself, I had to decide if I had the strength to attend a meeting that evening. I knew the meeting was important, but I was struggling. My soul was weary. I was mentally and emotionally drained. Talking to more people was the last thing I wanted to do. But my "keep on keeping on" attitude, drug me out the door to the meeting.

We start each Emmaus team meeting by sharing communion together. I was sitting in the chapel praying and just resting in God's peace as others arrived. I looked up and noticed the two candles on the communion table. One candle was dimly lit with just a small flame attempting to flicker. The other candle was beaming and glowing with a huge bright light. It was so intense my eyes continued to watch it flicker in the dimly lit chapel. As I watched the candles, I realized they can represent our walk with Jesus. We can be the dim light that barely shines for Christ when struggles come our way, or we can be the bright light which reflects Jesus in all circumstances. But then I realized that God was sending me a message. How would I handle Mom's diagnosis? I could allow the burden of my soul to diminish my flame for Jesus, or I could use this moment in my life to shine for Jesus. At that very hour I was surrounded by God loving, faithful, prayer warriors in this chapel. If I chose to share the burden of my heart, how precious each one of them would be to me as they stood in the gap with prayer. *1 Thessalonians 3:7–10* has become very real to me this week through my friends.

> *So we have been greatly encouraged in the midst of our troubles and suffering, dear brothers and sisters, because you have remained strong in your faith. It gives us new life to know that you are standing firm in the Lord. How we thank God for you! Because of you we have great joy as we enter God's presence. Night and day we pray earnestly for you, asking God to let us see you again to fill the gaps in your faith.*

There is nothing greater than the power of prayer to pull us through difficult times. I am thankful for each of my prayer warrior friends as I walk this difficult path with my parents.

Watching those candles made me realize that I need to let my light shine by sharing another story about Mom's doctor. This gentle, compassionate, humble man held Mom's hand as he gave her the news of the cancer. He kindly spoke comforting words of hope to us. God sent us an angel who compassionately ministered to us through this horrible news.

At one point he looked at my Mom and said, "Do you believe in God?" Mom replied, "Jesus too!" With sincerity and compassion he looked each one of us in the eye and said, "I am praying for you and your family." This wonderful doctor whom we have grown to love in the ups and downs of my parents' aging process, stepped into the gap as a prayer warrior for us as well.

God knew the road that was ahead of us and put His plan in place. Doc's compassion, prayers and love for my parents was the comfort we needed that sad morning. What an amazing God, that He cares so deeply for us that He even sent us a doctor who became our strength that morning.

BITTERSWEET CHRISTMAS

It is a bittersweet Christmas this year. It is a time of celebration for our Savior's birth. A time spent with friends, family, and great joy. But this year, Mom is no longer with us to celebrate. I have spent the last couple of days preparing for Christmas at Dad's house. That is where Christmas has always been, and where it will continue to be, but it will be very different this year.

The tree is up and decorated, but the wreaths aren't in the windows. The tables are set with the usual table clothes, but the china remains in the cupboard. The silverware has been replaced with plastic and tomorrow the eggnog may be served from the plastic carton, rather than a fancy pitcher.

It was a whirlwind illness for Mom just before Thanksgiving. There were only eight days from diagnosis to seeing Jesus. So tears may flow, but laughter will abound. The chaos of talking and endless chatter will fill the rooms as we start to reminisce of days gone by. But one thing will remain, and that is the joy of family as we gather together on Christmas day.

Joy is a word we so commonly use at Christmas time. The angel said, *"Don't be afraid! I bring you good news that will bring great joy to all people" (Luke 2:10).* We often sing, "Joy to the World, the Lord is come!" and "Joy to the World, the Savior reigns⸁!" But true joy is found on more than Christmas day. Joy is found when we seek and praise the Lord. *"Their hearts will rejoice with everlasting joy" (Psalm 22:26).* Most importantly, when troubles and sadness surround us, we can ask the Lord to *"Give us back the joys we once had!" (Lamentations 5:21).*

So on this bittersweet Christmas, my family and I will find joy in knowing that Mom was greeted by the Giver of all joy when she entered heaven's pearly gates. For *Isaiah 51:11* says, *"Those who have been ransomed by the Lord will return. They will enter Jerusalem singing, crowned with everlasting joy. Sorrow and mourning will disappear, and they will be filled with joy and gladness."*

AWAITING BABY KING

Our first grandson is due any day and we are so excited. About a month ago the doctor said he was going to be a big baby and maybe Kim wouldn't go full term. So for the last month we have waited impatiently. With every phone call or text message, I rush to answer thinking, "Baby alert?" But am disappointed when it isn't them. There is no baby yet, only false hopes that today is the day and life continues on as normal. Anticipation, excitement, curiosity, and concern are all rolled into one, as we await the arrival of Baby King.

Questions run through my mind. Will he look like Daddy or Mommy? How big will he be? What color hair will he have? Will he have blue or brown eyes? Will he have the same strong willed personality as his father? But concerns also run through my mind, so I pray.

> Lord, please keep him safe and healthy. I ask that
> you give Kim an uneventful and easy delivery. Lord
> you have blessed Baby King before he was ever born.
> You have given him wonderful parents, so continue
> to bless his life as well. Amen.

We have all of these concerns, questions, anticipation and prayers for our grandson who we will be holding in our arms soon. Can you imagine the thoughts of those who watched for the arrival of the true Baby King, the Messiah! Between the Old and New

Testaments there were no known prophets for over four hundred years. It appeared that God quit talking to the nation of Israel. They knew all the signs, yet no Savior appeared. I have impatiently waited this last month to meet our grandson, the nation of Israel waited over four hundred years to meet the King of Kings.

Christ's birth is prophesied in *Isaiah 9:6*. *"For a child is born to us, a son is given to us. The government will rest on his shoulders. And he will be called: Wonderful Counselor, Mighty God, Everlasting Father, Prince of Peace."* *Micah 5:2* told those watching for the Messiah that this Prince of Peace would come out of Bethlehem. *"But you, O Bethlehem Ephrathah, are only a small village among all the people of Judah. Yet a ruler of Israel, whose origins are in the distant past, will come from you on my behalf."*

There are many other prophecies in the Old Testament about the birth of Christ and His life which were to be fulfilled. Even the Samaritans who were not as knowledgeable about the prophecies of Christ were watching for the Messiah. In *John 4:25*, *"The [Samaritan] woman said, 'I know the Messiah is coming—the one who is called Christ. When he comes, he will explain everything to us.'"* Can you imagine the questions they had as they were awaiting the Baby King? The Pharisees and Sadducees were trained in the scriptures and had the most knowledge of the coming King, yet they denied that Jesus was the true Messiah. He challenged their manmade rules and regulations and their self-righteous ways. Jesus didn't come with the attitude of a religious King as they expected, instead He came as a servant to offer healing, compassion, and grace for both the Jews and Gentiles.

As expecting grandparents we will soon be blessed with our first grandson as our family continues to grow. But we are also blessed to be a part the family of God. A family that is open to all who accept the grace and forgiveness that Baby King Jesus offers to everyone. As I lay my head down at night I will not only pray for our Baby King, but I will pray to the King of Kings and thank Him for the grace and peace that He provides us each day.

REAGAN ELIZABETH

My youngest granddaughter is Reagan Elizabeth. When she was a baby, she could be a handful to babysit because she was Mommy and Daddy's girl. Our normal routine was to circle the house about once an hour to prove that they weren't home so she would quit fussing. Now that she is toddling around, she no longer cries when they are gone. But upon their return, she will always produce tears and wave her arms, fussing until one of them gathers her up into their arms for a hug.

We recently spent a few days together on vacation. In the middle of their trip, her daddy was out of town on business for a couple of days. He returned late one evening and the next morning she was so excited to see him. She remained very attached to him all day. He often travels for work, and this is her customary welcoming following each trip. Not only did she miss Daddy, but Daddy missed her. They spent the day together as she enjoyed playing, hugging and just sitting on his lap.

There are times in our lives when we feel like we have taken a trip from our heavenly Father. Less time in prayer and reading God's Word. Sin and shame cause a barrier. Worldly ways stand in the way of our closeness to God. Just plain overworked and under prayed can lead us to distancing ourselves from Christ. But upon our return home, our homecoming with Jesus will be just as glorious as it was for Reagan. Reagan's daddy didn't want to be away from her, nor does our heavenly Father want to be away from us.

James 4:6 tells us *"God opposes the proud but gives grace to the humble."* When we travel far away to the distant sinful land, God is still there circling and searching for us. Just as Reagan searches for her missing parents, His desire is to bring us back home to Him. No matter why we have traveled afar, we need to humble ourselves and ask for forgiveness. When we draw near to God once again, we will feel His wonderful presence.

James 4:9a says, *"Let there be tears for what you have done."* When James says we should shed tears, he is referring to tears of sorrow and deep regret. Tears for our sins which have built a barrier between us and Christ. When Daddy returns, Reagan also has tears. Obviously at ten months old, they aren't tears of sorrow for the sin in her life, they are joyful tears because he has returned. Like Reagan, I feel we should also cry tears of joy, for there is no greater feeling than the presence of the Holy Spirit returning into our lives. After all, *Psalm 68:4b* says *"Rejoice in his presence."* So why not cry when you return home from the distant land of sin!

In closing meditate on *James 4:10*, *"Humble yourselves before the Lord, and he will lift you up in honor."* I pray that you return from your sinful trip today and ask for forgiveness. Allow your heavenly Father to become your Daddy. He will sweep you into His arms, wipe away your tears, spend the day holding you, and lifting you up to a place of honor today.

Suggested Scripture Reading

- *James 4:1-10*
- *Psalm 68:4*
- *Psalm 59:9-10*

ULFILLMENT

We were blessed with a wonderful evening this week. Friends invited us to dinner. It was our choice of restaurant or she would cook at her home. So with my peanut butter fluff pie in hand, we joined them for dinner in their home. Not only was the food plentiful and wonderful, but the evening was so fulfilling (and more than just our bellies.) Being able to sit in the quietness of their home instead of a noisy restaurant allowed us to have heart to heart conversations about our lives. It was good for our souls and all part of God's timing in my life, as I have been leading the Bible study "Soul Keeping" by John Ortberg.

We were able to share the concerns of our hearts and the joys of our week. We discussed everything from the birth of our grandson, Jackson, to the ongoing illness of her father. The conversations ranged from joy, concerns, struggles, and sadness, but at the end of the evening there was such peace. Yes, they are great friends and it was a great evening, but this peace was much deeper than friendship. It was a peace that only the Holy Spirit can give you. As we parted for the evening, each of us knew that we were praying for one another. What a joy to know that our struggles, our concerns, our illnesses, and actually our entire lives are being lifted up by friends.

The book of James challenges us to live as Christians. It doesn't promise us an easy life, but convicts us to have faith in times of difficulties, and to persevere. The evening with our friends was a true example of what James asks of us at the end of his book.

Are any of you suffering hardships? You should pray.
Are any of you happy? You should sing praises. Are
any of you sick? You should call for the elders of the
church to come and pray over you, anointing you with
oil in the name of the Lord. Such a prayer offered
in faith will heal the sick, and the Lord will make
you well. And if you have committed any sins, you
will be forgiven. Confess your sins to each other and
pray for each other so that you may be healed. The
earnest prayer of a righteous person has great power
and produces wonderful results. (James 5:13–16)

Reread the last part of verse *16* again. *The earnest prayer of*
a righteous person has great power and produces wonderful results.
The evening with friends was about being able to help one another
through similar situations. When you can sit and share from your
heart and know that they once faced the same struggle, you feel
God's hand upon you as they offer advice. Not worldly advice,
but godly advice which is based on the wisdom they have already
obtained from walking the road ahead of you. No wonder we left
that evening feeling the peace and joy of the Holy Spirit! When you
couple the Christian advise of your friends, with their prayers, and
the biblical knowledge that the prayers of a righteous person produce
wonderful results, WOW! What peace and joy!

My challenge to you today is to tend to your soul by digging
into the book of James. Let God's Word resonate in your soul as you
read. Then invite some friends to dinner and allow the Holy Spirit
to lead you. In doing so, I pray that you will find true fulfillment
for your soul.

Peanut Butter Fluff Pie

4 oz. Light Cream Cheese, softened
1/2 Cup Peanut Butter
1 1/2 Cups Milk
1 Small Package Sugar-free Vanilla Pudding
1 - 8 oz. Carton Light Whipped Topping
1 Graham Cracker Pie Crust

With love, beat cream cheese and peanut butter together until
well blended. Slowly add milk and pudding mix. continue to beat
until fluffy. Fold in 1/3 of the whipped topping. Pour into pie
crust and chill. Top with remaining topping before serving.

Share with friends for complete fulfillment!

$\mathcal{T}$HE LOST SHEEP

> *Tax collectors and other notorious sinners often came to listen to Jesus teach. This made the Pharisees and teachers of religious law complain that he was associating with such sinful people—even eating with them! So Jesus told them this story: "If a man has a hundred sheep and one of them gets lost, what will he do? Won't he leave the ninety-nine others in the wilderness and go to search for the one that is lost until he finds it? And when he has found it, he will joyfully carry it home on his shoulders. When he arrives, he will call together his friends and neighbors, saying, 'Rejoice with me because I have found my lost sheep.' In the same way, there is more joy in heaven over one lost sinner who repents and returns to God than over ninety-nine others who are righteous and haven't strayed away!" (Luke 15:1–7)*

Over lunch one day my friend Angie asked how the book was coming along. I shared that I had written almost one hundred devotions and was going to stop there and send it to the publisher. She looked at me and said, "No, ninety-nine."

"Why ninety-nine?" I asked.

"Because of the lost sheep," she replied.

What an impact that simple statement had on my thinking and I quit writing devotions at ninety–nine. If you don't believe me, take the time to count the devotions and you will find that there are ninety-nine writings from the introduction through the conclusion. Why ninety-nine you ask? A reminder for you and me to pray for the lost sheep, because they are so precious to Jesus.

I recently watched the movie *War Room* and was so moved by the movie that I built my own war room in our basement. I have always believed in the power of prayer, but the portrayal in this movie ignited a new passion within me to not only increase my prayer life, but to pray more boldly. The room is simple, but just what I need to spend time alone with God. It is a mixture of old furniture to block the view of the furnace, an old area rug, a sheet to cover a bare wall, and a piece of fiberglass board which I use as a dry erase board. No money involved, very little time, a few decorations and a chair turned some useless space into a quiet room where I can pray.

You will find at the top of the dry erase board the words, "Lost Sheep." It is my reminder to pray boldly for those who are not walking with Christ. I ask God to move in their lives, that they may someday find Jesus. I pray God uses the stories and the words He has given me to reach the lost, and that this book will have an impact on their lives. Throughout the process of writing I have often wondered who would want to read my crazy stories. Along the way, many encouraged me to publicize them, and so I did. Writing devotions has become my passion and my form of journaling my thoughts. What I gained from this process far outweighs any time spent writing, because this book hasn't been about me or for me. This book is God's message to reach the lost. I am glad I persevered, because when one lost sinner turns toward Jesus, there is wonderful rejoicing in heaven.

Regardless of where you are in your walk with the Lord, please know that I am praying for you. I pray for the ninety-nine, asking God to help them remain bold in their faith so they may lead the lost one to the path of grace and forgiveness. And if you are the sheep who is lost, know that we may never meet this side of heaven, but you are always in my prayers. God loved you before you were formed, He loves you with all of your sins, and He loves you even more when you run into His arms of grace.

<u>Suggested Scripture Reading</u>

- *Psalm 139:13–16*
- *Matthew 9:9–13*
- *Romans 3:22–24*

CONCLUSION

This collection of devotions has been about one thing. Knowing Christ and growing closer to Him daily. Life is full of valleys, curves and bumps in the road. When we continually look for our Savior in the little things of life it gives us faith, hope, and love.

> *We don't yet see things clearly. We're squinting in a fog, peering through a mist. But it won't be long before the weather clears and the sun shines bright! We'll see it all then, see it all as clearly as God sees us, knowing him directly just as he knows us! But for right now, until that completeness, we have three things to do to lead us toward that consummation: Trust steadily in God, hope unswervingly, love extravagantly. And the best of the three is love. (1 Corinthians 13:12–13 MSG)*

I pray that you know Christ as your personal Savior and walk with Him daily. The devotion below was written by my son Ryan King when he was in college. With his permission, I share it with you in closing. If you do not fully understand what it means to be forgiven of your sins, I pray this simple description of sin and being washed as white as snow, will lead you one step closer to the Lord.

The Story of a Christian Farmer's Hat

Just about every farmer you will ever see has a hat on his head. We feel naked when we leave them at home and we just aren't comfortable without them. What started out as a simple cure for getting the sun out of your eyes, became an icon of American agriculture. Farmers express themselves with their hats or sometimes use them as bartering power by wearing a Case hat into a John Deere dealership. Either way, for a Christian farmer the hat means so much more.

A lot of us have that one cap that is super special. It is nasty, gnarled and just plain worn out. It looks absolutely trashy, and sometimes others comment on how filthy it is. But every day, the farmer wakes up, gets around, and puts on that dirty, smelly, undesirable old hat. My favorite happens to be an orange Alaskan Summer Ale ball cap. It is awfully dirty having been smeared with dirt, soybean dust, fish guts and many other foul things. Yet it is my most beloved of the collection, and I would never leave home without it.

While I was sitting in church holding the soiled hat in my hands, I had an awakening on the entire matter. That piece of fabric is really representative of sin. Sin is nasty, unclean and just plain looked down upon. No one wants to see it, do it, or even think about it. Yet every day we all do something sinful. Every day I pick up that same old stupid hat. So why do I put it on? Well why do I sin? I sin because I can't help it. I'm not a perfect person. None of us are. So from now on, I make that hat serve as more than just a head covering or an iconic image.

Whenever I put my favorite hat on my head, it is a daily reminder that sin is with me too. Just as some say that it makes me look stupid and filthy to wear the cap in public, so does sin.

So next time you head outside and reach for that hat, the one that hangs by the door, take a second look at how much dirt has covered the surface. Observe that it is faded and beaten with the stitches coming out. Then remember, you were the exact same way, right up until that wonderful day when you accepted the Lord as your Savior. Then I want you to go out the door wearing that hat with pride, because just like you, the cap is white as snow. It won't look perfect on the outside and sometimes the inside is equally as dirty. But you and that hat have been washed clean by the blood of Jesus Christ.

Ryan's example of the hat is something to which each one of us can relate. We all have some object that we cling to in spite of its worn out condition. For me it was a favorite pair of jeans. I loved those jeans and I was saddened when they finally were beyond repair and had to be pitched. But Christ doesn't pitch us just because we feel filthy, worn out, and gnarly. He loves us, forgives us, and we start each day anew in His eyes. As He promises in *Lamentations 3:22–23 (NIV)*, *"Because of the* LORD's *great love we are not consumed, for his compassions never fail. They are new every morning; great is your faithfulness."*

The following scriptures are God's promises to you. When He hung on that cross it was for your sins and mine. If it had only been for you, He still would have suffered for just you, because He loves you that much! As you read each verse, take a few moments to ponder, and understand how amazing Christ's love is. He faithfully forgives those who simply come to Him with a humble heart.

For everyone has sinned; we all fall short of God's glorious standard. Yet God freely and graciously declares that we are righteous. He did this through Christ Jesus when he freed us from the penalty for our sins. (Romans 3:23–24)

But if anyone does sin, we have an advocate who pleads our case before the Father. He is Jesus Christ, the one who is truly righteous. He himself is the sacrifice that atones for our sins—and not only our sins but the sins of all the world. (1 John 2: 1b–2)

For God so loved the world that he gave his one and only Son, that whoever believes in him shall not perish but have eternal life. For God did not send his Son into the world to condemn the world, but to save the world through him. Whoever believes in the Son has eternal life, but whoever rejects the Son will not see life, for God's wrath remains on them. (John 3: 16–17, 36 NIV)

Whether you know Jesus as your Savior or not, please pray the following prayer. God will hear you and forgive you of your sins.

Father, I know I am a sinner as filthy as a Christian farmer's hat. You are faithful every day and You wash my sins as white as snow. Your love and forgiveness are so amazing that as human beings we can't even begin to fathom the depths of them. Knowing that You suffered, died and rose again— just for me—gives me so much hope. Please forgive me of my many filthy sins Lord. Give me strength and understanding for each new day as I learn to daily seek Your will. Help me see that the valleys, curves and bumps in the road are signs of Your promises and the growth they bring. Help me to lean on Your understanding and walk with You, Lord. Father, You are my Savior, my Counselor, my Good Shepherd and my Friend. In Jesus name, Amen.

Let Jesus wash you white as snow and *Bloom Where You're Planted*.

ENDNOTES

a. Walsh, Sheila. *The Storm Inside: Trade the Chaos of How You Feel for the Truth of Who You Are.* Thomas Nelson, 2014.

b. "Broken Hallelujah - Mandisa | Song Lyrics | AllMusic." AllMusic. Accessed January 23, 2015. http://www.allmusic.com/song/broken-hallelujah-mt0031130354/lyrics.

c. "University of Wisconsin–Madison Biotechnology Center." Resources. Accessed January 11, 2015. http://www.biotech.wisc.edu/outreach/dnadance.html.

d. *The Bridges of Madison County.* [Warner Home Video ; [S.l.]., 1995. DVD.

e. *Pretty Woman.* Touchstone Home Video, 1995. DVD.

f. Gaither, Gloria. *Something Beautiful: The Stories behind a Half-century of the Songs of Bill and Gloria Gaither.* New York: FaithWords, 2007.

g. Brown, Robert K. *The One Year Book of Hymns.* Wheaton, Ill.: Tyndale House Publishers, 1995.

h. "I'm A Survivor [Album Version] - Reba McEntire | Song Lyrics | AllMusic." AllMusic. Accessed January 26, 2015. http://www.allmusic.com/song/im-a-survivor-album-version-mt0044687908/lyrics.

i. "The Heart of Worship - Michael W. Smith | Song Lyrics | AllMusic." AllMusic. Accessed February 3, 2015. http://www.allmusic.com/song/the-heart-of-worship-mt0006945821/lyrics.

j. "Worship."The Free Dictionary. Accessed January 23, 2015. http://www.thefreedictionary.com/worship.

k. "Raise Him Up - Randy Travis | Song Lyrics | AllMusic." AllMusic. Accessed January 23, 2015. http://www.allmusic.com/song/raise-him-up-mt0004650229/lyrics.

l. *Forrest Gump.* Paramount Pictures, 1994. Film.

m. "Scripture taken from the New Century Version®. Copyright © 2005 by Thomas Nelson, Inc. Used by permission. All rights reserved."

n. Brown, Robert K. *The One Year Book of Hymns.* Wheaton, Ill.: Tyndale House Publishers, 1995.

o. "Praise His Name - James Easter, Sheri Easter, Bill Gaither, Bill & Gloria Gaither, Gloria Gaither, Charlotte Ritchie | Listen, Appearances, Song Review | AllMusic." AllMusic. Accessed January 23, 2015. http://www.allmusic.com/song/praise-his-name-mt0003318392.

p. Burton, Valorie. *Successful Women Think Differently.* Eugene, Or.: Harvest House Publishers, 2012.

q. Scripture taken from the New King James Version®. Copyright © 1982 by Thomas Nelson. Used by permission. All rights reserved.

r. Brown, Robert K. *The One Year Book of Hymns*. Wheaton, Ill.: Tyndale House Publishers, 1995.

s. "Christian Quotes." Christian Quotes. Accessed January 11, 2015. http://christian-quotes.ochristian.com/.

t. Brown, Robert K. *The One Year Book of Hymns*. Wheaton, Ill.: Tyndale House Publishers, 1995.

About the Author

Mary resides in Radnor, Ohio with her husband, Jim. She is active in the Central Ohio Emmaus Community and the Richwood Church of Christ, where she is also employed as a part-time Administrative Assistant. Mary and Jim enjoy family, friends, traveling and farm life together.